Alexander's Buses

FIFE, MIDLAND, NORTHERN

Stewart J. Brown

Ian Allan
PUBLISHING

First published 2012

ISBN 978 0 7110 3552 2

Published by Ian Allan Publishing

an imprint of Ian Allan Publishing Ltd, Hersham, Surrey, KT12 4RG
Printed in England by
Ian Allan Printing Ltd, Hersham, Surrey, KT12 4RG

Distributed in the United States of America and Canada by BookMasters Distribution Services

Visit the Ian Allan Publishing website at
www.ianallanpublishing.com

Contents

Front cover **See page 61 top.**

Back cover (top) **See page 38 top.**

Back cover (bottom) **See page 47 top.**

Previous page **A contrast in Alexander-bodied AECs at Northern's Elgin depot, showing how much design had evolved in just two decades. Nearer the camera is a 1947 Regal 35-seater, with 108bhp 7.7-litre engine; alongside stands a new 1964 Reliance 41-seater with 126bhp AH470 engine, also of 7.7-litre capacity. The Regal would operate for 21 years, the Reliance for 15.** HARRY HAY

Foreword

ALEXANDER'S BUSES BECAME AN INTEGRAL part of our way of life in central and north-east Scotland. My father worked for the firm for 38 years, and I remember my excitement when in 1972 I was given a job as a bus conductor at the tender age of 18.

This book brings back many fond memories of what was always regarded as a very good bus service, and I am pleased to report that the tradition has been carried forward in the Stagecoach companies which succeeded many of these operations. In talking with some members of the Alexander family in recent times I realised how similar their foundations, business strategies and rapid expansion story were to our own experiences, and I am sure that you will find this detailed history a most interesting read.

Sir Brian Souter
STAGECOACH GROUP CHIEF EXECUTIVE

Above **Most of Sutherland's vehicles were single-deckers, and those that passed to the Northern fleet were mainly Leyland Tigers and AEC Regals. Heading back to Northern's Aberdeen depot in residential Gairn Terrace is a 1947 Regal with Brush bodywork, one of four. The depot site is now occupied by housing.** HARRY HAY

Introduction

IN 1961, W. ALEXANDER & SONS LTD was Britain's third-biggest bus operator, after London Transport and Midland Red. It operated a fleet of almost 2,000 buses and coaches covering a sizeable part of Scotland, from Glasgow in the south to Elgin in the north, and from Oban in the west to Aberdeen in the east.

Its blue buses operated urban services in Glasgow, the busiest with a nominal six-minute peaktime headway, backed up by scheduled duplicate buses, and operated by high-capacity 30ft-long 67-seat Leyland Titans. At the other extreme it ran prewar half-cab Tigers on remote rural services, some running just one or two days a week. The company's Bluebird coaches provided summer excursions from many of the towns it served, and operated seasonal express services such as those from Glasgow to Aberdeen and from Glasgow to Inverness. It took just over six-and-a-half hours to get from Glasgow to Aberdeen, including a 30-minute refreshment stop midway (where northbound and southbound crews changed coaches, allowing drivers and conductors to return to their home depots). Today the fastest journey takes 2 hours 40 minutes. A lot changes in 50 years.

The point is that Alexander's, as the company was generally known, was a diverse business covering every aspect of 1960s bus and coach operation at a time when car ownership was still low, and buses were, for most people, the only way to travel. There were around 750,000 cars on Scotland's roads in 1961; today there are 2.2 million.

The company had 41 depots plus a small number of outstations, and major workshops in Falkirk, Aberdeen and Kirkcaldy. It employed around 8,000 people. If that figure seems high by modern standards – four per bus – remember that every service bus carried a conductor or conductress. In 1960, the old company's last full year of trading, Alexander's made a pre-tax profit of £845,000, down from £1.1 million in the previous year. It was a big business.

Then, on 15 May 1961, it changed. Scotland's biggest bus company was divided into three. The division followed the lines of the company's existing area structure, the Fife and Northern Areas becoming W. Alexander & Sons (Fife) and W. Alexander & Sons (Northern). The Southern Area became W. Alexander & Sons (Midland). The Midland company also absorbed Alexander's Kirkintilloch-based subsidiary, David Lawson.

Above **Before adopting a cream roof as the standard style for single-deck buses, Northern repainted a few vehicles in this predominantly yellow livery, seen on a 1950 Tiger PS1 in Montrose, on the four-times-a-day service to Forfar. This yellow-roofed bus livery would be revived in 1977 for Y-type buses. The National Commercial Bank of Scotland, in the background, would be merged with the Royal Bank of Scotland in 1969.**
STEWART J. BROWN COLLECTION

At a time when the bus industry was fairly stable, this was a big event. The even greater upheaval which would be set in motion with the deregulation of local bus services, followed by privatisation, was still a long way in the future.

This volume tells the story of what happened to Alexander's after it was split into three, concentrating on the period from 1961 to privatisation. The opening chapter looks at the background of the company's remarkable growth, while the final chapter describes how, 50 years later, the Fife and Northern companies, along with part of what was Midland's territory, are united under the ownership of Stagecoach, while most of Midland's area is now served by First.

I've long had a soft spot for the Alexander's business. My first job, straight from school, was as a traffic apprentice with Midland, starting work at its depot in Stepps, north-east of Glasgow, in August 1963, and then in various other locations including its Camelon head office, its hires and tours office in Glasgow and, briefly, at the then new Cumbernauld depot. The company has gone. Stepps depot has gone; the site is now occupied by a Premier Inn. Of the other depots and offices I worked in, only Cumbernauld remains, now in the ownership of First Glasgow.

The Alexander's companies appealed to enthusiasts. The fleets were varied, and the vehicles were well maintained and well presented. I hope that in the pages that follow I capture some of the flavour of businesses which strove to provide a good and reliable service to their customers.

As a matter of style I've used 'Alexander's' to refer to the bus-operating company, W. Alexander & Sons Ltd, and 'Alexander' for the coachbuilding business, Walter Alexander & Co (Coachbuilders) Ltd. And in referring to one-man operation I'm using the language of the period. When driver-only operation was first being widely explored

in the late 1960s and early 1970s virtually all drivers were men. Indeed, it's interesting to note that as late as 1977 the Scottish Group Secretary for the Transport & General Workers' Union remarked in an interview that "the girls driving [buses] at the moment, in the main, have proved most satisfactory" and noted that at that time there were "more than 100 girls driving buses in Scotland". The gender-neutral concept of one-person-operation had yet to arrive, and I can only hope that his use of the term 'girls' didn't sound as patronising then as it does now.

My thanks go to Charlie Anderson, Gavin Booth, Iain MacGregor and Derek Stuart, who kindly read and commented on a draft of the text. Derek was a colleague of mine in Midland's Brown Street headquarters schedules office in the 1960s; he was later Traffic Manager of Northern and Managing Director of Fife, and after the Scottish Bus Group was privatised he ran the Oban & District company. Others who helped with information were David Toy, a former Chief Engineer of Northern; The Omnibus Society Library under the able management of Alan Mills; and *Buses* Editor Alan Millar, who made available the colour photographs of Jim Thomson. The work of Jim and other photographers who helped is credited individually where their names are known, but I've been collecting photographs of the Alexander's companies for the best part of 50 years, and some material comes from photographers whose names are not known. Stagecoach today covers the bulk of what was the Alexander's operating area, and I am grateful to Chief Executive Brian Souter for writing a foreword to this volume.

Stewart J. Brown
HEBDEN BRIDGE
NOVEMBER 2011

Left **The author's first workplace – the offices at Midland's Stepps depot – seen in August 1964. The Alexander-bodied Tiger Cub is ready to take up service on the route from Glasgow to Elgin. The 1946 Burlingham-bodied AEC Regal was one of the oldest buses at the depot. The depot engineer liked to leave it parked on the forecourt. If a driver of a bus from another depot was thinking of seeking a change of vehicle because of some minor defect, he'd be told to take the Regal which was standing ready to go. It dissuaded drivers from seeking changeovers, and saved the depot engineer the trouble of undertaking remedial work for another depot when he would rather be keeping his own vehicles in tip-top condition.**
STEWART J. BROWN

Scotland's Biggest Bus Company

Above **A new style of Alexander coach body was developed for the lighter underfloor-engined chassis which were becoming available in the early 1950s, and Alexander's took examples on Leyland Tiger Cub, Guy Arab LUF and Albion Aberdonian. There were 40 Tiger Cubs, 30 of which joined the Midland fleet, the balance going to Northern. They were new in 1954. This is one of the 10 coaches based in the Northern Area, seen in Tarland on an excursion to Dufftown. An Alexander-bodied Tiger PS1 stands in the background on the infrequent service from Tarland to Aberdeen which operated twice a day except on Fridays and Saturdays, when there were three trips.**
JIM THOMSON

WALTER ALEXANDER'S FIRST BUS WAS a charabanc with chain drive and solid tyres, built by Belhaven of Wishaw and purchased in 1914. It wasn't even a full-time bus. During the week it operated as a lorry, then at weekends was fitted with a charabanc body, running between Falkirk and Bonnybridge, a distance of five miles. The Alexander family owned a bicycle shop in Camelon, roughly midway between the two places. Such dual-purpose vehicles were not uncommon in the early days of bus operation. A second, similar, vehicle followed in 1916.

After the end of the Great War the family shop was sold, and the focus turned to running buses. The original route was extended west from Bonnybridge to Kilsyth – a further eight miles. The business, which had traded as Alexander's Motor Services, was in 1924 incorporated as W. Alexander & Sons Ltd, with its headquarters in Brown Street, Camelon. The fleet at that stage numbered around two dozen vehicles. The company reached south to Glasgow in 1924, and then north to Perth and on to Dundee.

This was a period of rapid expansion. Buses were becoming more reliable and were increasingly competing with rail services and, in towns such as Falkirk, with trams. Alarmed at the rapid growth of bus services, the railway companies started buying shares in bus companies. In Scotland the LMS and LNER companies bought into Scottish Motor Traction of Edinburgh in 1929, and SMT then took a major shareholding in the Alexander's business.

With the financial strength of the railway companies behind them, bus operators expanded even faster, both by opening new routes and by acquiring other companies. Significant expansion from 1929 included the setting up of Simpson's & Forrester's, which combined two separate businesses – Simpson's of Dunfermline and Forrester's of Lochgelly – which Alexander's had acquired. The S&F company had a short life, being formed in 1929 and then absorbed into the Alexander's business in 1938, at which time it ran 69 buses. Another 1929 acquisition was Pitlochry Motor Services, which operated as a separate subsidiary until 1942, with 11 vehicles, before being absorbed into the main fleet.

SMT bought the Scottish General group of companies in 1930, and these were integrated into the Alexander's fleet. The main business, the Scottish General Omnibus Co, based in Larbert, ran 183 buses. The former SGOC depot, locally known as Larbert Road, is today the site of the headquarters of First's Midland Bluebird business. Smaller businesses acquired with the Scottish General group were the Dunfermline & District Traction Co (33 vehicles), the Scottish General (Northern) Omnibus Co of Elgin (29) and Dunsire's Motor Service of Falkirk (10). The LNER's 35-bus operation in the North East was also acquired by Alexander's in 1930.

Thus by 1932 the Alexander's fleet numbered an impressive 800 vehicles (of which just 40 were double-deckers), and the company had operations as far afield as Elgin, Aberdeen, Angus, Fife and Glasgow. These 800 buses

Left **The last TS8s delivered to Alexander's before the war had 39-seat Alexander bodies. A Lawson example, one of seven in that fleet in 1961, heads to Glasgow on the circular service which linked the city with Kirkintilloch and Auchinairn.** IAIN MACGREGOR

were, to say the least, varied. Most were Albions and Leylands – around 350 of each – but the rest were a mixed bag of AEC, Bedford, Chevrolet, Clyde, Dennis, Gilford, GMC, Halley, Thornycroft and Tilling-Stevens models.

In the 1930s, Alexander's buses replaced trams in three towns – Kirkcaldy (1931), Falkirk (1936) and Dunfermline (1937). The company also became established as the city operator in Perth in 1934, when it took over Perth Corporation's 35 buses. Buses on local services in Perth and Kirkcaldy used a dark-red livery until 1961.

In the Glasgow area Alexander's strengthened its position in 1936 when it purchased the David Lawson business, based in Kirkintilloch. This, with a dark-red livery, remained a separate subsidiary until 1961, at which time it operated 89 buses and coaches. Its holiday coach tours operated as Lawson's Land Cruises, hinting at a touch of added luxury.

Alexander's coaches originally used the Royal Blue name, but that changed in 1934 with the adoption of the Bluebird name and a stylised bluebird logo; the name soon became synonymous with high-quality coach travel.

Leyland would quickly emerge as Alexander's preferred chassis supplier. From 1929, when the company bought its first Tiger, through to the end of normal peacetime deliveries in 1940, Alexander's took delivery of just over 1,000 new buses and coaches, of which 800 were Leylands. More than 200 of these Leylands were still in service when the three new Alexander's companies were created in 1961, by which time the oldest had been in service for 24 years. Their longevity is a tribute to Alexander's exceptionally high maintenance standards; even at the end of its life an Alexander's bus was still well looked after. At the time of the company's division, buses were repainted every 27 months, and preparing and repainting a bus in the Larbert Road paintshop took four days for a single-decker and five days for a double-decker. All of the work was done by hand.

The company had its own body-building facility, in Stirling, and this supplied the bulk of the bodywork for the company's buses in the 1930s, as well as producing bodies for other SMT-group operators. In the Alexander's fleet the principal exceptions in the 1930s were Bedford coaches, bodied by Duple of Hendon, and Leyland Titan double-deckers, which were supplied complete with Leyland's own side-gangway lowbridge bodies. Alexander would not build double-deck bodies until 1942, when a programme of rebodying Leyland Tiger coaches as double-deck buses was initiated. Just over 100 of Alexander's TS7 Tigers were rebuilt in this way, providing the fleet with added capacity to cope with wartime travel demands. In 1939, Alexander's operated 200 double-deckers, half of which were second-hand TD1 and TD2 Titans. When the war ended, the number of double-deckers in service had more than doubled, to 450, boosted in the main by the Tiger rebuilds and by the delivery of 101 Guy Arabs during the war years. In 1946, the

Below **A 1948 Leyland Tiger with 35-seat Alexander body typifies the early-postwar coach fleet. Between 1947 and 1950, Alexander's purchased 209 new Tiger PS1s, most with this style of body. They were later repainted in blue bus livery. The location is Crieff bus station.** JIM THOMSON

Right **Along with Leyland Tiger Cubs Alexander's also purchased AEC Reliances and Monocoaches. With a Lawson's Guy Arab for company, a Reliance stands in Glasgow's Parliamentary Road, having arrived on the service from Bo'ness. This style of 45-seat Park Royal bus body was fitted to 20 Monocoaches and 10 Reliances, all outwardly identical. A small number of Alexander's buses ran with cream roofs for a brief period in the late 1950s.** JIM THOMSON

Below **In 1960, for Highland coach tours, Alexander's took 10 Albion Nimbuses, four of which were allocated to the Lawson fleet. They had attractive 29-seat Alexander bodies which made full use of the developing technology of moulded glass fibre to create complex shapes for the front and rear of the coach – compare this Nimbus with the plain-looking 1957 model on page 29. A contemporary report on one of these coaches in the trade press spoke quaintly of the 'dignity of its interior finish'. Two of these coaches were transferred to Highland Omnibuses in 1965; the remaining eight ran for Midland until 1970.** STEWART J. BROWN COLLECTION

combined Alexander and Lawson fleet strength stood at around 1,220 vehicles, of which 1,000 were Leylands, and the most modern were 182 wartime buses – 101 Guy Arabs and 81 Bedford OWBs.

The involvement by the railway companies in part ownership of the SMT group and Alexander's in 1929 had been a significant event. Britain's railways were nationalised in 1948, responsibility for their control being assumed by the newly created British Transport Commission. The SMT group then decided to sell its bus businesses to the BTC, and so in 1949 Alexander's became a state-owned company. This had no immediate effect on the day-to-day running of the business, although it would have an influence on the company's vehicle policies. The coachbuilding business remained in the ownership of the Alexander family and would later be relocated from Stirling to a new factory in Falkirk; this opened in 1958 and is still building buses, now as part of Alexander Dennis.

There was further expansion in the early postwar years. SMT had local bus operations in the Dundee area. These,

along with 55 Leyland single-deck buses, were transferred to Alexander's in 1949. Then, in 1950, Alexander's purchased the bus business of Sutherland of Peterhead, which ran 82 vehicles in the Buchan area and on services to Aberdeen. It was a fairly modern fleet, and almost half of the buses acquired in 1950 – 38 – were still in service when the Northern company was formed in 1961.

Alexander's also became established in bus operation in Inverness, with the acquisition of local operator Greig at the end of 1947, to which it added the business of Wemyss of Ardersier in the summer of 1950. Greig operated 21 vehicles; Wemyss had seven. However, the company's Inverness operations were to be relatively short-lived, and the services, with 24 buses, were transferred to the new Highland Omnibuses business when this was set up as a BTC subsidiary at the start of 1952, primarily to take over the Highland Transport Co.

The scene was set for the rest of the 1950s. Alexander's was the only significant operator of local bus services in Fife. Outside the cities of Aberdeen and Dundee, where services were provided by municipally-run buses (and, until the middle of the decade, trams), it was the dominant operator in an area stretching from the River Tay to the Moray Firth. And in the Central Belt it was the main provider of bus services in Perth, Stirling, Falkirk and all areas in between. It also provided local services to the north of Glasgow, notably to Milngavie and, through its Lawson subsidiary, to Kirkintilloch, although the bulk of Glasgow's public transport needs were met by the trams, buses and trolleybuses of Glasgow Corporation Transport. And it served Oban, with a number of local routes and a twice-daily 100-mile-long service to Glasgow.

A measure of the importance of Glasgow to Alexander's operations can be judged by the number of timetabled departures from the city at the start of the 1960s. The company had three city termini, all within a few hundred yards of each other, with bus stations at Dundas Street and Buchanan Street (also known as Killermont Street)

and on-street loading at a terminus in nearby Renfrew Street. In a typical hour off-peak (between 1pm and 2pm) there were 68 departures spread between these three points, covering both local and long-distance services. In the evening peak (5pm to 6pm) this figure rose to an impressive 144, almost half of which left from Dundas Street – 70 buses in 60 minutes.

Throughout its vast operating area the company ran a comprehensive network of inter-urban and rural services, including links from Glasgow to Dundee, Leven, St Andrews, Callander and Crieff, and from Aberdeen south to Dundee and west to Elgin and Inverness. These services were in 1961 generally operated by Leyland Tiger Cubs and AEC Reliances. There were also holiday coach tours – 'extended tours' in Alexander's parlance – from Glasgow to destinations in Scotland and England.

At the start of the 1960s there were a few independent bus operators in the area served by Alexander's. The most substantial, working up from the south, were Carmichael of Glenboig, McLennan of Spittalfield, Greyhound of Arbroath and three Aberdeenshire businesses – Burnett's, Simpson's and Strachan's. Four of these six operators would be taken over by Northern and Midland in the middle of the decade.

In the rush to re-equip its fleet after the war Alexander's bought not only its preferred make of chassis, Leyland, but other types too – AEC, Albion, Commer, Daimler, Foden and Guy. In the 1930s, the company had bought small Bedford coaches for Highland tours, and it continued with this policy after the war. In the five years from 1946 to 1950, Alexander's took delivery of 635 new vehicles, almost half of which – 299 – were Leylands. The next-biggest suppliers were Guy (127) and AEC (92). Bedford delivered 41 of its classic OB model with Vista-style bodywork built in London by Duple and in Edinburgh by SMT. Examples of all of these chassis makes – apart from Foden – were still in service in 1961.

The BTC had substantial bus interests in England and Wales through its ownership of the Tilling group of companies, and this included two manufacturing operations – Bristol and Eastern Coach Works. This would have an influence on the SMT group's – and Alexander's – buying policy. The first sign of this was the use of ECW in 1951 to provide new double-deck bodies on five wartime Guy Arab chassis and also to build fully-fronted coach bodies on a batch of 13 new Daimler CVD6 chassis, creating a unique combination in the process. Alexander's first Bristol buses – 20 ECW-bodied LS6G models, allocated to the Fife Area – arrived in 1955, to be followed by double-deck Lodekkas from 1956. By 1961 there were 172 Bristols in the fleet – 152 Lodekkas and the 20 LSs. The Lodekkas introduced SBG's triangular destination layout to the Alexander's

fleet with a three-track route-number display above a single-line destination, and this would be the standard layout for double-deckers until the mid-1980s.

Apart from Guys delivered during and after the war most of Alexander's new double-deckers were of lowbridge layout, with a sunken gangway on the offside of the upper deck. This reduced the overall height from 14ft 6in to 13ft 6in. The advantage of the Lodekka lay in its innovative low-frame chassis, which allowed the bus to be built to the same height as a lowbridge model while retaining a central gangway on both decks. The standardisation on lowbridge or low-height buses was an operational convenience rather than a reflection of route restrictions. Alexander's, like other SBG companies, deemed it easier to have a universal standard for double-deckers, allowing them to be used on any double-deck route – unlike most operators in England and Wales, which were more inclined to buy lowbridge buses for specific services.

In 1952, Alexander's switched to the new generation of underfloor-engined single-deck chassis, taking 43 Leyland Royal Tigers alongside its last half-cab coaches, 20 Tiger OPS2s, which had been a cancelled export order and were no doubt acquired at an advantageous price. These would be followed by lighter-weight Tiger Cubs and AEC Reliances and Monocoaches. Guy supplied 20 Arab LUF coaches, and Bristol the one batch of LSs. Double-deckers were Leyland Titans (184 between 1950 and 1960) and the aforementioned Lodekkas, along with one batch of 20 AEC Regent IIIs.

This was the vehicle inheritance awaiting the three new companies.

The Great Divide

IN THE SPRING OF 1961, W. Alexander & Sons Ltd operated a fleet 1,937 buses and coaches, which was to be divided between the three companies which came into being on 15 May. The biggest was W. Alexander & Sons (Midland) Ltd, with 967 vehicles operating from 16 depots. Next came W. Alexander & Sons (Fife) Ltd, operating 516 vehicles from 11 depots. The smallest was W. Alexander & Sons (Northern) Ltd, with 454 buses and coaches, and 14 depots.

Midland retained the original Alexander's headquarters, at Brown Street, Camelon, as its head office. The new Fife company's base was at Esplanade, Kirkcaldy, while Northern's head office was originally at the depot and divisional workshop in suburban Gairn Terrace, Aberdeen, but moved to the company's new £80,000 bus station in Guild Street when that opened in 1963. A bus station had been sadly lacking in Aberdeen and, prior to its opening, Alexander's services had five different departure points inconveniently spread around the city, none of which offered any passenger facilities or easy interchange between services. The new bus station was adjacent to the city's railway station, offering smooth transfer between bus and rail services. When it opened it was handling just over 230 departures a day.

The biggest depots had allocations of around 120 vehicles – Larbert, Milngavie and Stepps in Midland; Dunfermline and Kirkcaldy in Fife; and Aberdeen in Northern. The biggest double-deck fleet by a significant margin was based at Milngavie, which had around 90 Leyland Titans. The next-biggest concentrations of double-deckers were in Fife, both Dunfermline and Kirkcaldy having around 70. The smallest depots typically had around a dozen vehicles – Oban and Pitlochry in the Midland company, and Newburgh and St Andrews in Fife – while Northern's smallest allocations were at Fyvie and Huntly, each with just six vehicles.

All vehicles carried a small cast plate indicating the depot to which they were allocated. Before 1961 these were coloured blue for Southern Area buses, green for those in the Fife Area, and orange for Northern Area buses. The code was the first letter of the town – P for Perth, for example – or the first and last letters where the first letter was already in use; thus Pitlochry was PY. The depots are listed in Appendix 2 on page 96.

Throughout the 1950s, Alexander's had in the main been buying Leyland Titans and Tiger Cubs, AEC Reliances and Monocoaches, Bristol Lodekkas and Bedford coaches, along with small numbers of other types. Vehicles with

Above **Buses used on town services in Kirkcaldy and city services in Perth shared the same red livery and in 1961 had broadly similar fleets made up of Guy Arab IIs and Bristol Lodekkas. Here the conductor of a Perth Guy confers with his driver. New in 1944, the Guy had a 56-seat Northern Counties body. The last of the Guys employed on Perth city services were replaced by new blue-liveried FLF Lodekkas in 1963.**
IAIN MACGREGOR

Left **Most of the 101 Guy Arab
III single-deckers purchased
by Alexander's between 1946
and 1949 operated in the Fife
Area. A 1948 bus with 35-seat
Brockhouse body is seen
in Kirkcaldy in 1962. It was
one of 20, all of which passed
to the new Fife company.**
IAIN MACGREGOR

Gardner engines were concentrated in the Fife Area, in the Lawson fleet, and in the Perth City Services fleet, which was made up largely of wartime Guy Arabs. When Gardner-engined Bristol Lodekkas started arriving in 1956 they were allocated not only to traditional Gardner depots in Fife (including eight in dark-red livery for Kirkcaldy town services) but also to depots in Stirlingshire – Grangemouth, Larbert, Stirling and Bannockburn – that had not previously operated Gardner-powered buses. There were 27 in the Lawson fleet at Kirkintilloch and nine in the red-liveried Perth City Services fleet. The only vehicles with horizontal Gardner 6HLW engines were 20 Bristol LS6Gs and 20 Guy Arab LUFs, and these were all based in Fife. There were no Gardner-engined buses in the Northern Area.

Alexander's AECs were shared between the Northern and Southern Areas. Just as there were no Gardner-powered buses north of the River Tay, there were no AECs in Fife. Thus in 1961, both Northern and Midland were running Regals, Reliances and Monocoaches. There were also 20 Regent IIIs in the Midland fleet, dating from 1951 and operating in the Stirling and Falkirk areas. Northern had two Regent IIIs, with unusual lowbridge Massey bodies, acquired from Sutherland of Peterhead and still based at the former Sutherland depot in the town.

Albions had figured prominently in Alexander's early days – there were around 350 in 1932, making up 44% of the fleet. Albion's slogan was 'Sure as the sunrise', but, 30 years on, the sun appeared to be setting for Albion at Alexander's. There were just 44 in operation in 1961. Most

of these were Aberdonians (a poor man's Leyland Tiger Cub), and although there were but 23 they were divided between all three companies – 17 with Northern, five with Fife and just one with Midland. The Aberdonian had a derated (94bhp) version of the 108bhp O.350 Tiger Cub engine and an Albion five-speed gearbox. There were also 15 Nimbuses, all of which went to Midland, and five Victors, all in Fife. The Victors were odd coaches, with Strachans bodies and petrol engines; they were the only petrol-engined vehicles in the Fife fleet. The Nimbuses were used mainly on tours to the Highlands, and eight were in the Lawson fleet. The Nimbuses formed the N class; the Aberdonians were NL (Nimbus Long). The final Albion was

Below **The first ECW
double-deck bodies
for Alexander's were
replacements for wartime
utility bodies on six Guy Arab
chassis. Five of these were in
the Lawson fleet in 1961 and
would operate for Midland
until 1965. In this evening
view one heads back to its
Kirkintilloch base. Lawson's
routes were numbered
in their own series, from
170 to 180.** IAIN MACGREGOR

Above **Glasgow's Dundas Street bus station in the late 1950s, with an Alexander's Bristol LS6G departing for Leven. This service ran every two hours and from 1961 would be a joint operation between Fife and Midland, requiring two buses from each company. Although a 45-seat bus, the Bristol originally wore Bluebird coach livery and is seen here fresh from its first repaint, when it received the more appropriate bus colour scheme. On the left of the LS can be seen a Lawson Lodekka, and behind it a prewar Tiger, waiting to leave for Annathill. The route number should read 27, not 270.** JIM THOMSON

Right **The low bridge in Dunnikier Road in Kirkcaldy has claimed many double-deck victims over the years, and this notice was on display in Fife's Kirkcaldy depot with what might be called a blunt '3D' warning: Danger, Dunnikier Road, Dismissal. It is illustrated with pictures of buses cut out of a 1950s magazine and was still in situ in the mid-1970s.**
STEWART J. BROWN

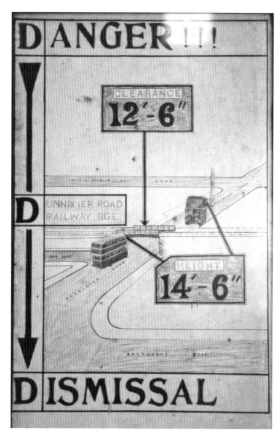

a solitary Valkyrie with much-rebuilt bodywork by Walker of Aberdeen. New in 1946, it had come with the Sutherland business and spent its life in the Northern Area.

In the late 1940s, Alexander's had bought small petrol-engined coaches for its touring fleet – 41 Bedford OBs and 28 Commer Commandos. Nine of the OBs survived in 1961, shared between Midland and Northern. There were also nine Commers, with bodywork – unusual for the time in having an aluminium structure – by Scottish Aviation of Prestwick, and these all passed to Midland, including two from the Lawson fleet. Both types were soon to disappear.

Daimler was another minority make. There were 36 CVD6 coaches, all but four of which were at Southern Area depots and passed to Midland; the odd four were in the Northern Area. And there were 13 CWA6 double-deckers. Three, delivered new in 1944, spent their entire 20-year lives at Grangemouth. The other 10 were Northern Area buses acquired from Sutherland, and all would be transferred south to Midland in 1962. The transfer of buses between Alexander's companies after 1961 was never very common; the movement of 17-year-old buses nearing the ends of their lives was extremely unusual.

Leylands made up the bulk of the Alexander's fleet in 1961. There were 1,039 of them, equal to 54% of the fleet. The list of models read like a Leyland historical catalogue. In order of age there were Cheetahs, Tigers of types TS7, TS8, TS11, PS1 and OPS2, Titan models TD4, TD5, TD7, PD1, PD2 and PD3, plus Royal Tigers and Tiger Cubs.

Given the high proportion of Leylands in the fleet it was inevitable that they would be spread throughout the three companies. The main exception was the lack of any PD1s or PD3s in Fife. Alexander's had started taking 30ft-long PD3s in 1958, following on from batches of PD2s and, before that, PD1s. The PD1s and PD3s were shared between Midland and Northern; there were PD2s in all three of the new companies. Unusual among the PD3s were 17 described as PD3/3C models, built in 1960. These vehicles used new Leyland chassis frames into which Alexander installed the running units – O.600

engine, gearbox, axles – from eight-year-old PB-class Tiger OPS2s. It was originally intended that all 20 PBs should be used for double-deck conversions, but in the end only 17 were done. They were the company's last new buses with exposed radiators. All were allocated to the Southern Area and therefore passed to Midland. The OPS2s which provided the running units for the PD3/3Cs were in turn fitted with engines, gearboxes and axles from withdrawn PS1s. This made them less powerful, 100bhp 7.4-litre engines replacing the 125bhp O.600s. And the use of 7ft 6in-wide axles in coaches that were 8ft wide also made the rebuilt OPS2s look over-bodied. The three OPS2 Tigers that retained their original engines operated for Fife.

The older single-deck Leyland Tigers and the Royal Tigers were spread across all three of Alexander's operating areas. The newer Tiger Cubs were divided mainly between Midland and Fife, with just 10 (out of 202) in the Northern Area. Most of the Northern Area's single-deckers from the mid-1950s had been AECs. The Tiger Cubs, 1954 coaches, were based at Aberdeen and Dundee.

The oldest vehicles to be taken over by the new companies dated back to the latter half of the 1930s. There were 1937 Leyland Tiger TS7s at Fife and Northern, 1938 Cheetahs at Fife and Midland, and TS8s from 1939/40 running for all three companies. Most of the TS8s had been built to a design with a modified driving position which allowed the front bulkhead to be slightly further forward than on a standard chassis, making room for an extra row of seats to give a seating capacity of 39.

The oldest double-deckers – discounting wartime rebuilds of 1930s Tiger chassis – were a 1937 Titan TD4 at Fife, 1939 TD5s at Midland and 1940 TD7s at Northern. The last prewar buses would be withdrawn by Fife and Northern in 1963 (TS7s and TS8s), and by Midland in 1964 (TS8s and rebodied TS7s).

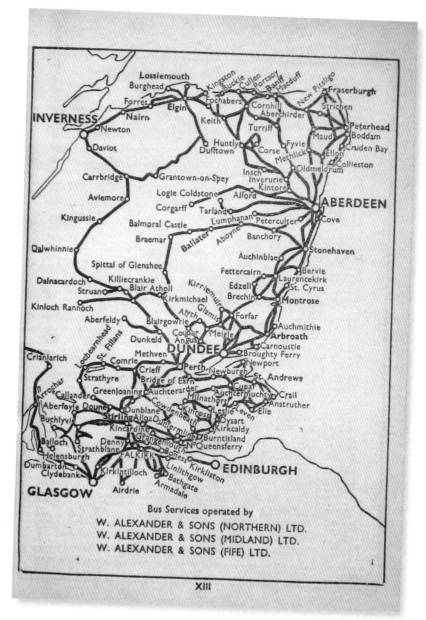

Bus Services operated by
W. ALEXANDER & SONS (NORTHERN) LTD.
W. ALEXANDER & SONS (MIDLAND) LTD.
W. ALEXANDER & SONS (FIFE) LTD.

XIII

Left **The only petrol-engined vehicles in the Fife fleet were five Strachans-bodied Albion Victor 29-seat coaches, which had been ordered by two operators in Devon but were instead bought by Alexander. New in 1950, they received the new cream-and-red Fife coach livery and were operated until 1964.**

IAN ARMSTRONG

Above **The area covered by the three Alexander's companies is shown in this map, which appeared in early-1960s timetables and was an update of a much older map. It omits Oban, which lies off the map, to the west of Crianlarich.**

STEWART J. BROWN COLLECTION

A Decade of Change

3

AT FIRST THE ONLY OUTWARD sign of the creation of the three new companies was a change to the legal lettering on the sides of the vehicles. Then a few buses started to receive a modified version of the distinctive W. Alexander & Sons fleetname, to which was added the Fife, Midland or Northern name as appropriate. This arrangement lasted for less than 12 months, and early in 1962 new fleetnames and liveries were announced. Midland retained the established azure blue and cream. On most double-deckers there was one band of cream relief below the lower-deck windows, while single-deck buses had a cream waistband. Coaches were cream with a blue roof and waistband, although that changed on new deliveries from 1962 to cream with blue window surrounds and waistband. Fife adopted Ayres red and cream, initially applied in the same layout as had been used for the previous blue. Most strikingly, Northern's new livery was yellow. A few buses were repainted using the traditional Alexander's livery layout, but Northern then experimented with alternative layouts, incorporating more cream, before settling on the use of cream lower-deck window surrounds on double-deckers and a cream waistband and cream roof for single-deck buses.

With the new liveries came attractive new script Fife, Midland and Northern fleetnames, with different styles for buses and coaches. The fleets were also renumbered, but

only by adding an F, M or N prefix to the existing fleet number. The detail of the numbering system is explained in Appendix 1 on page 94.

The short-lived W. Alexander & Sons (Midland) Ltd fleetname appeared on a few red-liveried Lawson buses, but with the announcement of the new fleetnames and liveries it became clear that the Lawson identity would disappear. So too did the use of dark red for city-service buses in Perth, which became blue, and town-service buses in Kirkcaldy, which adopted the same brighter, Ayres red as the rest of the Fife fleet. To avoid confusion, now that all buses in Kirkcaldy were going to be red, the words 'Town Service' were displayed on a board on the fronts and sides of vehicles running on Kirkcaldy local routes – an arrangement which lasted until the late 1960s. The good citizens of Perth were left to identify local services by their route numbers.

The Bluebird name, synonymous with Alexander's coaching operations for more than a quarter of a century, disappeared, although all three companies initially continued to use the bluebird symbol on the sides (and often backs) of coaches. Indeed, history would prove the bluebird to be a particularly resilient creature.

Renumbering and repainting was effected with considerable speed. Midland, of course, had simply to apply new fleetname transfers to its blue buses. Repainting

Above **When the new Fife company adopted a red livery, buses used on town services in Kirkcaldy initially carried a 'Town Service' board on the front to distinguish them from other red buses. This 1959 Bristol Lodekka LD6G was one of eight in Kirkcaldy which had been in town-service red. Lodekkas of this vintage had a 16-year operational life.** IAIN MACGREGOR

Left **Among the oldest vehicles acquired by Midland were 60 Leyland Tiger TS8 Specials, supplied to Alexander's in 1939/40. The 'Special' referred to the revised driving position, which was more upright than on a standard chassis and thus enabled the cab to be shorter and the front bulkhead to be moved forward by about six inches. This increased the seating capacity from 35 on standard TS8s to 39 on the modified vehicles – an increase of 10%. This bus, seen in Glasgow in 1963, wears its age lightly and is indicative of the high standard of presentation that was a characteristic of Alexander's vehicles.**
STEWART J. BROWN

at Fife included wartime Guys but excluded soon-to-be-withdrawn prewar vehicles, just one – a 1939 Tiger TS8 – gaining Fife's cream-and-red coach livery. Used on tours which crossed the River Forth on a ferry which could not accommodate a full-size coach, it operated until 1963, by which time it was the oldest bus in the fleet and was used as a back-up for a coach-liveried PS1 – the only half-cab PS1 in any of the three fleets to receive coach livery, although the PB-class OPS2s were initially painted in coach livery by Fife and Midland.

At Northern a few prewar Tigers were repainted yellow (as buses, not coaches), while the oldest double-deckers to be repainted were 1948 Leyland PD1s. Northern's oldest double-deckers – 16 Leyland TD7 Titans from the early 1940s and 10 ex-Sutherland Daimler CWA6s – were all out of the fleet by the start of 1963 and remained in blue until the end.

The creation of the new companies also brought about joint operation on a small number of long-distance services, primarily between Glasgow and Fife. Thus from 1962, red-liveried Fife Bristol LSs and Tiger Cubs could be seen in Glasgow on services from Dunfermline, Leven and St Andrews. There was joint operation between Midland and Northern on the Glasgow-Dundee service, which meant that once a day a yellow Northern bus, usually an AEC Reliance, appeared in Glasgow. There were in addition seasonal long-distance limited-stop services which became joint operations, primarily between Midland and Northern and linking Glasgow with Dundee and Aberdeen. Midland buses appeared frequently in Dundee on services from Perth, but only in the summer months did they reach Aberdeen.

One summer-season service, from Glasgow to Inverness and Elgin, was advertised as being operated jointly by Midland and Northern but was in fact a pure Midland operation. It included an overnight journey that was operated by one coach making northbound and southbound trips on alternate nights – north on Mondays, Wednesdays and Fridays and south on Tuesdays, Thursdays and Saturdays. The night service was scheduled at 6 hours 20 minutes to Inverness, with a 30-minute refreshment break in Perth. The day service, which had more stops and a 50-minute lunch break at Dunkeld northbound or Pitlochry heading south, took 7 hours 25 minutes.

At the start of the 1960s, Scotland had no motorways and only limited stretches of dual-carriageway trunk roads in the area served by the Alexander's companies,

Below **Before adopting new liveries and fleetnames the new companies for a short time used a modified version of the traditional company name, as shown on a Fife bus.**
STEWART J. BROWN

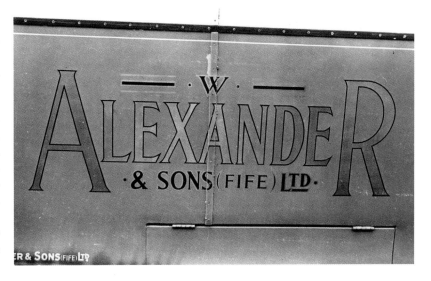

Above **Late wartime survivors in the Midland fleet were two Willowbrook-bodied Leyland Tiger TS11s dating from 1942. Based at the company's Kilsyth depot, they made regular appearances in Glasgow on the Saturdays-only service from Twechar via Muirhead. They were withdrawn in 1964, the year this one was photographed in Dundas Street bus station.**

HARRY HAY

most notably on the A80 between Stepps and Denny. As a result, long-distance services still passed through large and small towns, making for slow journeys.

Deliveries to all three companies in 1961 were vehicles ordered prior to the split, and all were supplied in Alexander's blue livery. These were Tiger Cubs for Midland and Fife, Leyland Titan PD3As for Midland and Northern, and Lodekkas for Midland. The first sign of Northern's independence was that its seven PD3As were registered in Aberdeen rather than in Stirlingshire.

The Midland Tiger Cubs were 19 stylish coaches which used the standard Alexander body shell but featured attractive new glass fibre front and rear mouldings and had glazed cove panels. They had 38 rather than 41 seats, a one-piece inswing door in place of the standard jack-knife unit, and a revised livery of cream with blue window surrounds. (The prototype – which brought the total to 20 – appeared initially in overall blue but was repainted cream before entering service.) So they were true touring coaches rather than the dual-purpose vehicles beloved of Alexander's and other Scottish Bus Group companies.

The step forward represented by the 38-seat Tiger Cubs can best be measured by comparison with the new touring coaches for the Lawson fleet, delivered the previous year. These were Reliances which had standard dual-purpose Alexander bodies with one row of seats removed, making them 37-seaters. This, and the use of a better-quality seat, was a gesture to comfort, but by no stretch of the imagination were they first-class coaches.

The first year in which the new companies were free to follow their own vehicle policies was 1962. For double-

deckers Midland and Fife continued buying Lodekkas but switched to the high-capacity FLF with 70 seats – 10 more than the LD model which had preceded it in Alexander's orders. These were the first forward-entrance double-deckers in both fleets and were Fife's first 30ft-long double-deckers. The 12 for Midland were based at Perth, where they replaced Guy Arabs on city services. All three companies also placed orders for the new low-height Albion Lowlander, which was conceived as a replacement for the lowbridge version of the Titan PD3. Although badged as an Albion and assembled in that company's Glasgow factory, the Lowlander was really a Leyland. It used the same O.600 engine as the PD3 – and retained that model's driving position, which was relatively high for a low-height design. This made for an awkward seating layout at the front of the upper deck. The PD3s had been 67-seaters; the Lowlander, with forward-entrance Alexander body, seated 71. For Midland and Northern, operators of PD3s, the move to the Lowlander was logical. It was a bit of a surprise at Fife, which had last received new Leyland double-deckers – PD2s – in 1953, since when Lodekkas (80 of them) had been the only double-deckers allocated to the Fife Area.

All three companies' Lowlanders – which arrived late, at the start of 1963 – had semi-automatic Pneumocyclic gearboxes, a first. The Midland and Northern fleets had a few Daimlers and AECs with pre-selector gearboxes, while every bus in the Fife fleet had a manual gearbox, so the semi-automatic Lowlanders marked a major change. The seven for Fife – allocated to Cowdenbeath for use on the service between Dunfermline and Ballingry – were to be its last new Leyland-engined double-deckers. The two Lowlanders delivered to Northern would be not only its last new Leyland-engined double-deckers but also its last new double-deckers of any description for 18 years. When new they were the only forward-entrance double-deckers north of Perth, being based in Aberdeen and initially operated alongside PD3s on the busy cross-city service between Culter and Dyce. Only Midland placed a repeat Lowlander order – before its first batch was delivered – and ultimately took a total of 44, all delivered in 1963. The following year Midland tried an AEC Renown demonstrator, operating it from Larbert Road alongside Lowlanders on the service between Falkirk and Glasgow via Kilsyth, as well as on Falkirk local services, but no orders ensued.

Midland had earlier evaluated two Daimler Fleetline demonstrators at Grangemouth depot. The first, with Weymann body, was tried in 1962, to be followed in 1963 by a Northern Counties-bodied bus. As with the Renown, neither of the Fleetlines produced any orders. It would be 1967 before rear-engined double-deckers joined the fleet.

The Lodekkas and Lowlanders were delivered in the three new companies' liveries. The Lodekkas for Fife and Midland had two cream relief bands, the standard Alexander's layout for the model. The Lowlanders for Fife, and the first batch for Midland, had a single band of cream

Left **Most of Alexander's Guy Arab III single-deckers were in Fife, but there were also 22 in the Lawson fleet, and in 1961 these passed to the new Midland company. This ex-Lawson bus, with 35-seat Massey body, is seen at the former Lawson's depot in Kirkintilloch in May 1962, soon after being repainted blue and before receiving the new script Midland name. A Duple-bodied Guy, still in Lawson's colours, stands in the background.**
STEWART J. BROWN COLLECTION

relief below the lower-deck windows (this having been the standard layout on Alexander's Titans). The low floor level and low window line of the Alexander body on the Lowlander left little space for the relief band as it crossed the rear wheel-arch, and Midland's second batch of Lowlanders arrived with a Lodekka-style livery layout; the earlier vehicles were later repainted to match. Northern was still deciding on a livery for its double-deckers, and its Lowlanders were yellow with cream window surrounds on both decks and a cream roof. The roof and the area around the upper-deck windows was quickly repainted yellow, and this livery – yellow relieved by cream around the lower saloon windows – became the Northern standard for double-deckers, remaining so until 1985.

In the early 1960s a number of bus operators experimented with illuminated exterior advertising on double-deck buses, with a large panel on the offside of the vehicle in which advertisements were back-lit by fluorescent tubes. Midland specified illuminated panels on 24 of its Lowlanders, and both of Northern's were similarly equipped. The panels were striking at night but failed to generate an increase in revenue sufficient to justify their being fitted to any subsequent new vehicles. In the middle of the decade both Midland and Northern introduced exterior advertising on single-deck buses, using the cove panels. This allowed advertisers to reach customers in areas not served by double-deckers (Oban and Pitlochry, for example), but few advertisers took advantage of the opportunity.

Another surprise at Fife in 1962 – bearing in mind that there were no AECs in the fleet – was an order for 12 AEC Reliances. Repeat Reliance orders would be placed in 1963, 1964 and 1966, by which time there would be 59

in service. The first 12 had BET-style 41-seat Alexander bodies. Eight similar vehicles were delivered to Northern, along with 10 which used the same body shell but were fitted with 45 bus seats. Although service buses, they were in coach livery. The use of coach livery on new single-deck buses would be a feature of deliveries to Midland until 1971 and Northern until 1975.

Midland stayed loyal to the Tiger Cub and ordered 20. The first 19 entered service in 1962 and had the same BET-style 41-seat body as supplied to Fife and Northern on Reliance chassis, but with detail differences in the specifications. This depended on whether they were intended as touring coaches or dual-purpose vehicles; some had one-piece manual doors, others had powered jack-knife doors, and there were different destination layouts too.

Below **Alexander's painted underfloor-engined buses in coach livery when they were new – a policy that seems to undermine the association between the Bluebird name and luxury travel. This is a 45-seat Alexander-bodied AEC Reliance in Elgin bus station in 1962, with a freshly repainted Northern-liveried bus in the background.**
STEWART J. BROWN COLLECTION

Above **Fife's elderly Guy Arab IIs were generally confined to local services. However, the Glasgow Fair holiday created tremendous demand for transport to holiday destinations, including the Fife coastal resorts, which saw all types of vehicles making the trip from Glasgow. This Guy was 19 years old when photographed in Glasgow's Parliamentary Road in July 1965. Most Fife Area routes, apart from the Kirkcaldy and Dunfermline town services, were numbered in the 300s, and this bus is showing route number 314, reflecting its usual duties on the frequent service between Dunfermline and Ballingry.**

HARRY HAY

The final surprise in the first orders placed by the newly independent companies was that each company took four Bedford VASs – three coaches with attractive 29-seat Duple Bella Vista bodies and one rather agricultural bus with 30-seat Duple Midland bodywork. There were at this time no Bedfords in the Fife fleet. The buses were being tried as a way of keeping costs down on rural services, but just one more VAS bus was purchased – by Northern, in 1964 – so it is reasonable to deduce that the VAS was not the answer to the problem of running cost-effective rural routes. The VAS coaches were more successful, all three companies placing further (small) orders: Midland added another six coaches in 1963, Fife one in 1964; Northern would take six in 1968, and Midland a final seven in 1970. The 1962 VASs for all three companies were the last vehicles to be delivered to Fife and Northern in Alexander's blue-and-cream livery. They were quickly repainted.

There were vehicle transfers between Northern and Midland in 1962, involving the 10 Daimler CWA6s mentioned earlier and four Leyland Titan TD7s. These were the only such transfers between the two companies, although in the 1970s there would be some vehicle movements in the opposite direction. These elderly vehicles had short lives with Midland; all had gone by the end of 1964.

There were few independent bus operators in the area served by Alexander's, and the first acquisition of an independent by one of the new companies came in the spring of 1962, when Midland purchased the business of

McDougall of Oban. This company ran seven Bedfords – six coaches and a bus – but none was used by Midland, even though four of the Bedfords were just two years old. McDougall operated tours and a once-a-day service between Oban and Easdale. This consolidation of Midland's position in the town saw its depot there being given its own code – ON – and vehicle allocation; it had previously been run as a sub-depot of Stepps, 100 miles distant. Midland's Bedford VAS bus was allocated to Oban when new, mainly for use on the Easdale service.

One peculiarity of the Oban operations was the summer service to Ganavan Sands, for which there were different timetables for 'inclement weather' and for better days when a more frequent service was provided 'weather permitting'. Other services with a similar caveat were operated by Northern between Banff and Tarlair Swimming Pool, 'weather permitting and according to traffic requirements', between Montrose Square and the beach, and from Arbroath to Elliot (Caravan Site) which operated 'when the Bathing Pool is open, according to traffic requirements'. Fife had similar summer local services in Anstruther and Leven but with no such meteorological limitations; perhaps hardier holidaymakers headed to Fife.

The three companies' timetable booklets were of a standard SBG style, with a blue cover to reflect the Alexander's livery. In 1961, the titles on the cover changed to show the new company names. Then, in 1965, there was a revamp of timetable design nationwide under the auspices of an organisation with the weighty title of the British Omnibus Companies Public Relations Committee. This saw most major operators throughout the country adopt a standard page size, a standard typeface, standard codes to indicate days of operation and the 24-hour clock. The new timetables were a substantial improvement over those that had gone before, with greater clarity of information. At this point the timetable covers were redesigned to incorporate a drawing of a Y-type coach, and with a colour to match each company's livery. There

TIMETABLES

Alexander's timetables spelled out in detail rules for the conduct of passengers, set by regulations dating from 1936. In 1961, these included some quaint instructions, including that passengers should not 'enter or alight from the vehicle otherwise than by the doors or openings provided for the purpose'. In addition, a passenger must not 'when in or on the vehicle to the annoyance of any other persons use or operate any noisy instrument or make or combine with any other person or persons to make any excessive noise by singing, shouting or otherwise'. And, most curious of all, was the instruction when on a vehicle not to 'throw any money to be scrambled for by any person on the road or footway' – something it is hard to imagine any bus passenger wishing to do, although presumably it had been enough of a problem in 1936 for it to require regulation.

would be a further cover redesign in 1973, featuring an updated Y-type, but the internal layout of the timetables continued unchanged, although they did now include the few services run by other operators.

The big event in 1963 was the arrival of the Alexander Y-type. Set aside its long-term influence on the Scottish bus scene over the three decades that followed and look just at its immediate impact when the first examples were delivered to all three Alexander companies on AEC Reliance chassis and, additionally, on Tiger Cubs for Midland. The first Y-types entered service as the last prewar buses were being withdrawn. And even compared with the coaches delivered just 12 months earlier they represented a remarkable advance. They had curved-glass windscreens and panoramic side windows with forced-air ventilation in place of traditional opening windows. (The forced-air ventilation wasn't an unqualified success, as it depended on the driver switching on the motor to power the fans, but that doesn't detract from the concept as being a good idea.) Little did anyone realise that for the best part of 20 years most of the single-deck buses and coaches purchased by Fife, Midland, Northern and other SBG companies would be Y-types of one sort or another.

In 1963, Midland took five Y-type Reliances (its last AECs), along with 22 Tiger Cubs. Fife had 14 Reliances, Northern, 22. A further 18 would join the Northern fleet in 1964.

Other 1963 deliveries included more Lodekkas – 70-seat FLFs for Midland, but 60-seat FS6Gs for Fife, marking a return to rear-entrance buses after 1962's Lowlanders and FLFs. Fife would take a second batch of FSs in 1964; these were the last new rear-entrance double-deckers for

an Alexander's company. Ten FLF Lodekkas for Midland in 1964 would be that company's last new half-cab double-deckers.

What was to prove an even more significant Y-type development appeared in the Midland fleet in 1964 – a

36ft-long version based on the Leyland Leopard PSU3/3R chassis with manual gearbox. There were fifteen 49-seat coaches, which were used on inter-urban services, and fifteen 53-seat buses with conventional short windows incorporating hopper ventilators in alternate bays. Although out-and-out buses, the 53-seaters were delivered in coach livery. These new Leopard buses had the same number of seats as the early-postwar double-deckers they were replacing and could – in theory at least – carry 24 standing passengers. They started a new MPE class, which would ultimately, 25 years later, reach MPE459.

There was in the early 1960s some nervousness about the use of 36ft-long vehicles. Their use had been legalised

in 1961; the previous length limit had been 30ft. Before ordering 36ft Leopards, Midland had borrowed a 36ft Reliance from Scottish Omnibuses to check its suitability for use on selected day excursions, ensuring, for example, that it could negotiate the winding roads used by tours from Glasgow which skirted Loch Lomond. Midland also evaluated a 36ft-long AEC Reliance demonstrator in 1963. Based at Grangemouth depot, it was used on local services and on the Bo'ness-Glasgow route, presaging the introduction of 36ft Leopard coaches to this route the following year. Another inter-urban route which benefited from the arrival of the Leopard coaches was that from Edinburgh to Stirling, Crieff and Callander – the last-named being a 50-mile trip which took just over 2½ hours.

Fife also embraced the 36ft-long Y-type, but on AEC's Reliance chassis. It took six 53-seat buses in 1964, along with six 49-seat coaches and seven short-length 41-seat coaches, similar to those delivered in 1963. Unlike Midland, Fife chose to paint its 53-seaters as buses. It also modified its coach livery in 1964, substituting cream for red on the roof, which made the vehicles look much brighter. This livery, cream with a red waistband, was applied to older coaches as they were repainted, among them, surprisingly, some of the Tiger OPS2s.

Midland's 1964 Y-types included its last Tiger Cubs, concluding a 10-year association with the type, and taking the number of Tiger Cubs to just over 200, making it the most common type, accounting for 20% of the fleet. With the last Tiger Cubs came a solitary Viking VK41L, on loan from Albion. This, unlike the VK43L that followed it, had a front-mounted engine and a set-back front axle. This layout – later popularised by Ford with the R-series –

allowed passengers to board opposite the driver. The engine was a vertical version of the Leyland O.370, derived from the O.350 fitted to the Tiger Cub, and was coupled to an Albion five-speed constant-mesh gearbox. The 41-seat bus had been exhibited in Midland livery at the 1963 Scottish Motor Show and entered service at Perth in August 1964, numbered MN16 at the end of the MN-class Nimbuses. Weighing just under 5½ tons, it was around half a ton lighter than a Tiger Cub. It ran until January 1965 and was then returned to Albion. Like the smaller Bedford VAS before it, the VK41 was not the rural bus that the company was seeking. Midland then briefly ran a West Yorkshire Road Car Bristol SUL4A with 36-seat ECW body on the Falkirk-Dunfermline service but was not impressed. The SUL4A used the same four-cylinder 4.1-litre Albion EN250 engine as was fitted to the company's 10 newest Nimbuses so presumably looked like a potential successor to the little Albions.

In 1965, all three former Alexander's companies introduced to their fleets a brand-new model – the rear-engined Albion Viking VK43L. This featured a vertical Leyland O.400 driving through a five-speed constant-mesh gearbox – a combination that required some driving skill on a vehicle not equipped with anything as frivolous as a rev-counter. There were 37 in total – 15 for Northern, 12 for Fife and 10 for Midland. Engine intrusion reduced the area available for seating at the rear, and standard Vikings were 40-seaters – one seat less than on an equivalent Tiger Cub or Reliance, despite being 2ft longer. The engine position precluded the fitting of a conventional rear luggage boot, but the Vikings had side luggage lockers, and the raised platform above the engine was also on occasion used for luggage. Eight of the Vikings for Midland were 34-seat touring coaches, as was the first for Fife. These were equipped with public-address equipment and had a half-height (rather than full-height) partition behind the driver.

The Viking can perhaps best be seen as an interesting side-track in bus history. A wry observation in a 1965 issue of the monthly magazine *Bus & Coach* noted: 'The Viking VK43L chassis looks curiously like a front-engined model in which the engine, radiator and gearbox have, by some dreadful mistake, been fitted at the wrong end.' It would feature in Midland's orders until 1969, by which

time the company had 75. Fife, too, bought Vikings until 1969, building up a fleet of 48, including eight fitted with 43 bus seats while retaining panoramic windows – a unique specification for an Alexander's company. Northern built up Britain's biggest Viking fleet, having 88 in service by 1970, including a former Leyland development chassis which had a Pneumocyclic gearbox; it would later increase this total to 94 (amounting to 20% of its fleet), acquiring six coaches from Scottish Omnibuses

in 1972. Forty-six Vikings delivered to all three companies in 1966/7 had bodies built in Belfast by Potter, predecessor of the Alexander (Belfast) bus-building business, although these were indistinguishable from coaches built in Alexander's Falkirk factory.

But the bigger story in 1965 was the delivery of 52 Leopards with 49-seat Y-type bodies to Midland, introducing added comfort to more of the company's trunk routes. It was to be the biggest single batch of new vehicles in Midland's history and represented a significant improvement in vehicle quality, the stylish heavy-duty Leopards replacing Tiger Cubs and Reliances on long-distance services. Four similar vehicles were delivered to Northern; to speed delivery Northern received vehicles that had actually been intended for Midland.

Fife had ordered 14 Bristol FLFs for delivery in 1965, but these were diverted to Central SMT, which in turn released 18 two- and three-year-old Albion Lowlanders which were sent to Fife, where they joined the seven 1962 buses at Cowdenbeath depot. Two had Alexander bodies, similar to Fife's own Lowlanders, but the rest were bodied by Northern Counties, which builder's approach to bodying the Lowlander was more elegant than that of Alexander, with a neater seating arrangement around the front upper deck. Most entered service in Central livery before being repainted in Ayres red.

There was expansion of Fife's operating area in the 1960s, thanks to the opening of new bridges across the rivers Forth and Tay to replace ferry services. The Forth

Left **Midland acquired most of Alexander's Daimler CVD6 coaches, operating them initially in coach livery. However, in 1965, shortly before they were withdrawn, eight were repainted as buses, as seen on this coach on a private hire in Glasgow's George Square. It had a 35-seat Burlingham body. The combination of bus livery and the Bluebird logo – rather than the Midland fleetname on the side – was unusual. The client for such an elderly coach was the Scottish branch of the Omnibus Society.** HARRY HAY

Road Bridge opened in September 1964 and prompted Fife to introduce services running to Edinburgh from Dunfermline every half hour via two routes, as well as from Leven and Kirkcaldy running to a co-ordinated timetable, hourly from the former and half-hourly from the latter. There were also Saturday services from Glenrothes to Edinburgh and one round-trip on Saturdays from St Andrews. The St Andrews service aside, all of the new routes were operated jointly with Eastern Scottish, so as well as introducing red buses to Edinburgh they brought green buses to Fife. When the bridge was first opened, the 2s 6d (12½p) toll was paid by the conductor using money from his or her cash bag. The services were an instant success and carried almost 750,000 passengers in the first six months of operation.

The new Forth Road Bridge also resulted in Northern's established summer service from Aberdeen to Edinburgh being re-routed. This had previously headed south from Perth via Stirling and Falkirk; the opening of the bridge saw it running by way of Kinross and Cowdenbeath, the end-to-end journey time being thus reduced from 6½ hours to just 5 hours. A truncated Falkirk to Aberdeen service was retained on summer Saturdays. The building of the bridge also led to the introduction a new service between Perth and Edinburgh, operated jointly by Midland and Eastern Scottish, each company providing one round-trip per day. This service ran via Turnhouse Airport at Edinburgh, where it provided connections with British European Airways flights to and from London. In those less security-conscious

days the transfer time allowed between the arriving coach and departing aircraft was just 25 minutes.

There was further expansion for Fife in August 1966, when the opening of the Tay Road Bridge provided the opportunity to start new services to Dundee. Thus red buses could for the first time be seen regularly north of the Tay. Fife's two established services from Leven to Tayport on the north Fife coast – one via St Andrews, the other via Cupar – were diverted to serve Dundee, as was the service from Kirkcaldy to Newport. The running time from Leven to Dundee was the same as that to Tayport, where there had previously been connections with a cross-river ferry that operated half-hourly. Fife also introduced a new Tayport-Dundee service, while Northern introduced a service between Dundee and Wormit, in North Fife. In what looks like the laziest possible example of the scheduler's art, the services from Dundee to Tayport and Dundee to Wormit had a running time of 15 minutes with three minutes' layover in Dundee and one minute in Tayport or Wormit. This gave a frequency of a bus every 34 minutes. Clearly an easily memorised timetable was not a high priority.

There were a few small operators in Fife. One, Fleming of Anstruther, which ran four coaches, was bought by Fife in

Below **The opening of the Forth Road Bridge prompted the introduction of new services linking Fife and Edinburgh. This is the cover of the original timetable for the new routes.** STEWART J. BROWN COLLECTION

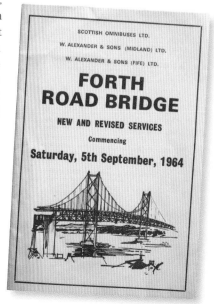

SCOTTISH OMNIBUSES LTD.
W. ALEXANDER & SONS (MIDLAND) LTD.
W. ALEXANDER & SONS (FIFE) LTD.

FORTH ROAD BRIDGE

NEW AND REVISED SERVICES

Commencing

Saturday, 5th September, 1964

Above **The 74 Alexander-bodied Leyland Royal Tigers purchased in 1952/3 were impressive coaches and were to be found in all three fleets. Their centre-entrance layout made them relatively inflexible, and while they would occasionally be used on local services they were more often to be found on private hires or long-distance routes. The lower-case fleetname dates this photograph to some time after 1968, meaning the coach was at least 15 years old when operating a private hire in Helensburgh. But it was still immaculate, and the seats are even fitted with antimacassars. These coaches weighed 7 tons 16cwt – heavier than many of the company's double-deckers – and had vacuum brakes whose effectiveness in the 1960s was often criticised by drivers used to more modern, air-braked coaches.** HARRY HAY

At Fife the five odd petrol-engined Albions were withdrawn in 1964 when 14 years old. This was at a time when some vehicles in the Fife fleet had 20-year operational lives, but 14 years wasn't at all bad for a non-standard light-duty chassis. Their withdrawal marked the end of the operation of petrol-engined vehicles by Fife. The last petrol-engined coaches in the Midland and Northern fleets – Bedford SBs – were taken out of service in 1967 and 1968 respectively. No matter how smooth and quiet they were, petrol-engined coaches were much more expensive to run than diesels. All of these Bedfords had Burlingham bodies, and three in the Midland fleet were luxurious touring coaches with two-plus-one seating for 24 passengers, offering a standard of armchair comfort combined with near-silent progress which was never to be seen again.

As they aged, the centre-entrance Leyland Royal Tigers delivered in 1952/3 were often to be found on bus work, usually, but not necessarily, on longer-distance routes. Even though virtually all buses were still crew-operated in the 1960s, the centre-entrance layout was not ideal for service work, and all three companies carried out forward-entrance conversions of Royal Tigers in 1965/6. Midland converted two, Northern three, and Fife rebuilt five of the 11 it owned, among them two Leyland-bodied coaches. The conversions did not extend the vehicles' lives; all of Fife's Royal Tigers were withdrawn in 1970/1, as were most of Midland's; the majority of Northern's went in 1972. In the early 1960s Midland reversed the livery on its Royal Tigers, then reverted to the original layout on repaints later in the decade.

The original script 'Midland' fleetname had a short life. Introduced in 1962, it was replaced in 1965 by a new block-letter fleetname which echoed the old Alexander style, incorporating 'W. Alexander & Sons' above the word Midland and 'Limited' below it. A simplified version was used on some coaches. This new fleetname was also short-lived, and in 1968 was replaced by a simple lower-case 'Midland'. The double-deck livery was improved too, from 1964, additional bands of cream relief for the company's AEC Regents and Leyland Titans creating a new standard double-deck livery, with either two or three cream bands depending on body style.

Acquisitions featured prominently in 1966. The first, in August, saw Midland acquire the business of Carmichael of Glenboig, which traded as Highland. Carmichael operated services between Coatbridge, Moodiesburn and Kilsyth and in Cumbernauld New Town, as well as running contract services for the coal mines which were major employers in the area. The company's livery was red and cream.

Carmichael ran what might politely be described as a mixed fleet of 30 vehicles, ranging from elderly Albion Valkyries to modern Leyland Leopards. All were allocated fleet numbers by Midland, creating a new MNA class for the old Albions, and an MPF class for five former Glasgow Corporation Leyland Worldmasters. Fifteen vehicles were repainted blue – two Aberdonians, six Leopards, the ex-Glasgow Worldmasters,

the spring of 1965; all four vehicles were sold without being operated. A more significant acquisition was that by Northern of Strachan's Deeside Omnibus Service of Ballater, in May 1965. Strachan's operated services between Aberdeen and Braemar and Ballater, starting from a stance in Dee Street, just off Union Street. The company ran 12 single-deckers, including seven Fodens, a rebodied Leyland Tiger PS1 and four AECs, in a livery of red, cream and black. The newest vehicle was 11 years old, the oldest 18 – but, despite their age, Strachan's vehicles were smartly turned out. All received fleet numbers (on paper, at least), the Fodens creating a new NF class. Ten of the Strachan's vehicles were withdrawn almost immediately, and only two received Northern livery, these being the PS1 and a Reliance, which were operated until 1969 and 1973 respectively.

Northern operated Scotland's biggest fleet of Albion Aberdonians, numbering 17 examples. This total was increased to 20 in 1965 with the acquisition of three eight-year-old coaches from Western SMT, in which fleet they had been non-standard. Aberdonians would run for Northern until 1975.

The arrival of new vehicles in all three fleets was, of course, matched by the withdrawal of old ones. Midland's entire fleet of Daimler CVD6 coaches – there were 32 – was withdrawn in 1965. The newer ECW-bodied coaches retained Bluebird coach livery to the end, but a few of the Burlingham-bodied coaches had been repainted in predominantly blue bus livery shortly before withdrawal. Other types to disappear from the Midland fleet were the last of its AEC Regals, by then 18 years old, in 1965, and in 1966 the last Guy Arab III coaches, which by now had been running for 20 years – most of that time in the Lawson fleet.

a Duple-bodied Tiger Cub and a Titan PD3 with forward-entrance Alexander body, bought new by Carmichael in 1962 for its Cumbernauld town service. The PD3 had been built as a stock vehicle for Millburn Motors, the Glasgow-based Leyland dealer, to a similar specification to buses being delivered to Glasgow Corporation.

Repainting of the fleet was a drawn-out process, and not until 1969, with the withdrawal of an ex-Ribble PD2 (after three years in Midland ownership), was Carmichael's red livery finally eradicated. Meanwhile the operation was transferred to a new depot in Cumbernauld, opened in January 1968 to replace Carmichael's rather basic premises at Greenfoot Garage in Glenboig. During its time with Midland (1966-74) the ex-Carmichael PD3 was the company's only highbridge bus. The last ex-Carmichael buses were withdrawn by Midland in 1975. For a brief period after the Carmichael acquisition the Midland fleet topped the 1,000 mark. The new Cumbernauld depot also took on some workings on services which ran through Cumbernauld to Glasgow.

At the end of 1966 the focus of attention switched to Northern, when it agreed the acquisition of the two biggest independents in its operating area, Simpson of Rosehearty and Burnett of Mintlaw, which between them operated 45 vehicles. The Simpson's takeover was completed in December, the Burnett's acquisition at the start of January 1967.

Simpson's ran 31 buses and coaches, in a green-and-cream livery, operating from Aberdeen to the Fraserburgh area and running local services in Fraserburgh and in Forres, the latter a separate operation 70 miles from the company's main base. Here too, all of the vehicles were allocated fleet numbers, four Ford Thames Traders starting a new NT series (T for Thames, as Ford coaches

were usually described at that time) – an unlikely beginning for a class that would ultimately number more than 200 vehicles. Early withdrawals included the only ex-London Transport RT-type AEC Regent to be operated by an Alexander's company, and assorted Leyland Royal Tigers and Bedford and Ford coaches. Only six vehicles were repainted in Northern livery – two ex-Yorkshire Traction double-deck rebuilds of 1947 Leyland Tigers, with handsome highbridge bodies built in 1955 by Roe, and the four newest Ford coaches, which dated from 1964/5. The double-deckers were operated until 1971, the Ford coaches until 1976.

Burnett's was a smaller operation, running 14 vehicles, all of which were AECs, in a smart livery of two shades of

Above **Ten of Alexander's Royal Tigers had Leyland bodies – a cancelled order which no doubt meant they were secured at an attractive price – and these were operated by Fife and Northern. A Northern coach stands in Glasgow, having arrived from Aberdeen on one of the two limited-stop services that connected the two cities.** HARRY HAY

red and cream. It operated services from Aberdeen to Stuartfield, Maud and Turriff, sharing with Simpson's a terminal in the city's Mealmarket Street. There were also Turriff-area local services. The Burnett fleet had a greater number of modern vehicles than did Simpson's (and was, perhaps, better maintained), and in consequence nine were repainted yellow – five Reliances, three ex-City of Oxford Regent IIIs and an ex-City of Oxford Regal III. The Regal III was withdrawn in 1972 and was the last half-cab single-decker in SBG service. The last ex-Burnett vehicles were withdrawn in 1976.

Later in 1967, Northern made what would be its last major acquisition, that of Mitchell of Luthermuir. This business operated services in the Luthermuir and Brechin area with 11 second-hand single-deckers including three Bristol LWL6Bs – a rare type in Scotland – and various Tiger Cubs, Ford coaches and a Guy Arab LUF. The three Tiger Cubs and four Fords were repainted in Northern livery and were operated until 1972. The Bristols and the Guy, which

created new NE and NGA classes, were withdrawn in Mitchell's colours in 1969/70 but did display their Northern fleet numbers on a small disc in the windscreen.

Finally, in 1968, Northern took over operation of the Stonehaven town service – a short trip to Brickfield – operated by Invercarron Garage, which ran about once an hour. No vehicles were involved.

There were two small takeovers by Fife in 1967. One Bedford coach was acquired from Niven of St Andrews, which had operated a local service in the university town. New in 1963, it was operated by Fife until 1972 when it was withdrawn along with the company's five VASs, bringing an end to Bedford operation by the company. Three vehicles were taken over with the business of Drysdale of Cupar; none saw service with Fife.

Following the acquisition of Lowlanders from Central SMT in 1965, further second-hand vehicles gravitated to the Fife fleet in 1966/7. There were another 14 Lowlanders, but this time from Western, which also supplied two older

vehicles – a 1949 Leyland Titan PD1 with a 1952 ECW body and a 1954 rebuild of a London Transport wartime Guy, which had a lowbridge Northern Counties body and a Birmingham-style 'new look' front. The Guy was operated in Western livery; the others were repainted in Ayres red. The PD1 was the only example of this type to operate for Fife. It was numbered in the FRB class of PD2s, although technically it should have been an FRA.

Central supplied two 14-year-old Guy Arab III double-deckers – a type familiar in the Fife fleet – and two 18-year-old Leyland Titan PD2s. The PD2s ran until 1968, the Arabs until 1970 – which was to be the last year of double-deck Arab operation by Fife. An intriguing might-have-been, also acquired from Central but not used, was a one-time London Transport RTL-type Leyland, which Central had taken over in 1961 with the business of Chieftain of Hamilton. It got as far as being allocated a fleet number – but no further.

Delivered in the summer of 1967 were the last new half-cabs for Fife – 18 FLF Lodekkas with an extended rear overhang which provided space for an extra row of seats, increasing capacity from 70 to 76. They were the company's biggest buses and would remain so until the delivery of 77-seat Daimler Fleetlines in 1971.

Alongside further Albion Vikings and Leyland Leopards, Northern's 1967 intake of new vehicles included an Austin Princess Vanden Plas seven-seat limousine. This was for an innovative service which used

the recently opened Tay Bridge to provide a link for Dundee-area businessmen (and women) with Edinburgh's Turnhouse Airport for British United Airways flights to London. Numbered NX1, the Princess was operated in black – a yellow limousine would surely not have appealed to sober-suited Dundonians – but did carry headboards promoting the service.

The closure of rural railway lines under the Beeching programme affected many parts of Scotland in the 1960s but had little impact on the Alexander's companies. Most of the lines had irregular services which were little used. The

Beeching report cited the Gleneagles-Crieff-Comrie service with 10 trains a day on which there were never more than an average of five passengers on a train at any given time. When the rail service was withdrawn Midland introduced three return trips daily between Crieff and Gleneagles. Very often the Alexander's companies were already providing bus services to the communities whose trains were being withdrawn, as, for example, on the line from Aberdeen to Ballater, which closed in 1966, and there was little or no need to revise timetables when the trains stopped running. Elsewhere there were short-lived replacement services. When Dullatur station, on the line between Edinburgh and Glasgow, was closed Midland provided a peak-time bus service for commuters, linking Dullatur with trains at Cumbernauld station. Little used, it was soon withdrawn. Longer-lived services were introduced by Midland between Stirling, Callander and Crianlarich when that rail line closed in 1965, with five trips a day, two of which provided direct connections at Crianlarich station with trains to or from Oban. Rail closures were an emotive topic in the 1960s – almost 100 stations in the Alexander's companies' operating areas were listed for closure – but in many rural areas the trains had lost out to competing buses long before Dr Beeching appeared on the scene.

In Perth, Alexander's out-of-town services departed from street stances – the main ones being in the forecourt of the railway station and on Tay Street, by the side of the river of the same name which runs through the city. Perth's first bus station, similar to that in Aberdeen, but smaller, opened in Leonard Street, a short walk from the railway station, in the summer of 1966 and was a starting-point for services operated by all three Alexander

companies. It catered for long-distance and country services but was not used by Midland's city services. In the understated way of the times, a press announcement noted: 'Without fuss or ceremony Perth's new Bus Station swung quietly and effectively into operation.' The same statement advised that the bus station was 'admirably situated' and had 'tastefully decorated' crew rooms. From Perth, Fife ran services to Kirkcaldy, Dunfermline, Leven and St Andrews, while Northern operated to Dundee, Forfar and Blairgowrie. Midland covered all other areas.

Parcels were long a part of Alexander's business, the importance of the traffic varying greatly between locations, and a feature of most of the companies' bus stations was a parcels office. In the mid-1960s there were just over 350 parcel agents listed in the companies' timetable books – 90 in Fife, 96 in Midland and a massive 168 in Northern, reflecting the rural nature of Northern's operations. Most were newsagents or grocers, but the more quaint included Mr A. Melville, blacksmith, in Collessie (one of four blacksmiths in Fife who acted as parcel agents), Mr Clark, a saddler, in Edzell and Mr Fairlie at the Regal Cinema in Nairn, whose parcels were no doubt delivered by Regals at the start of the decade. In Callander the agent was the Stirling Co-op Society boot department. The network read like a gazetteer of Scotland, if not from A to Z then certainly from Aberchirder to Woodside, and many agents were in hamlets which you would be hard-pressed to find on a map.

On the vehicle front, horror stories about poor reliability and high maintenance costs had seen SBG companies approach rear-engined double-deckers with considerable caution. The first for one of the Alexander's

Left **For many years Alexander's bought Bedford touring coaches. These included 10 petrol-engined SBG models with Burlingham bodies, delivered in 1956, which in 1961 would be shared between Midland (which got eight) and Northern (two). The Midland vehicles were withdrawn in 1967, ending the operation of petrol-engined coaches by the company. This one is making a stop in Helensburgh while on a Loch Lomond & Trossachs tour.** HARRY HAY

businesses were ordered by Midland for delivery in 1966 but did not enter service until the start of 1967. These were 20 Daimler Fleetlines, and they had Alexander's attractive double-deck body, technically the D-type, although seldom referred to as such. It was low-height, of course, and used the same windscreen as was fitted to the Y-type. The front upper-deck windscreen was the same as the rear window of the Y-type – a quite remarkable achievement in making use of common parts without compromising the styling of either model.

The Fleetlines were 75-seaters – at that time Midland's biggest buses – and were originally crew-operated. Double-deck one-man-operation (the gender-specific terminology of the time) was legalised only in 1966, and then it was up to operators to secure agreement with the trades unions. They were the first new Daimlers for Alexander's since CVD6 coaches in 1951.

A further 25 Fleetlines were on order for 1967, and these arrived later in the year, in a bright new livery with cream window surrounds on both decks and a cream roof. Sadly, the bright new look did not win approval, and the buses were fairy soon repainted in standard livery. The first were treated in the summer of 1968; all had been done by 1970. Another 25 Fleetlines were delivered in 1968. Although it had ordered Fleetlines, Midland tested a Leyland Atlantean demonstrator, with Park Royal body, at Milngavie depot in the spring of 1967. As the company's new standard double-decker the Fleetline could soon be found at most of the company's depots; by the early 1970s almost all those operating double-deckers (the exceptions being Alloa, Bannockburn and Stirling) had an allocation.

Midland's front-line coaches were early-1960s Tiger Cubs, and in 1967 the company initiated a major upgrade of its coach fleet when it took delivery of 15 Bedford VAM5s with 45-seat Duple Viceroy bodies. Northern would buy two similar coaches in 1968, but on the more powerful (150bhp) VAM70 chassis, which had replaced the 105bhp VAM5, a further four being delivered in 1970. The Midland VAMs introduced a new Midland Bluebird fleetname, which would be used on Duple-bodied coaches (but not any other types) until 1978.

Fife followed Midland's lead in selecting the Fleetline as its new-generation double-decker – it was in effect the SBG standard – and took its first 20, with Alexander bodies, in 1968, 14 more following in 1970. The first eight Fleetlines were allocated to Kirkcaldy local services but without the 'Town Service' boards which had hitherto been used to distinguish town buses from country buses. There were no new double-deckers for Fife in 1969; instead it bought a dozen elderly Lodekkas, new in 1955, from Central. As with some of Fife's previous acquisitions from Central, these ran initially in their previous owner's livery. They were retained for three years.

Below **In 1957, Alexander's purchased five Albion Nimbuses with 29-seat Alexander bodywork, four of which were allocated to the Lawson fleet. This coach, seen in Glasgow's Dundas Street bus station in 1965, was based at Oban, whence it had arrived on a service usually operated by Tiger Cubs. At this time a small bus such as this, working a largely rural service, would still have carried a conductor. In 1966, it and two similar vehicles would be transferred to Crieff for use as one-man buses on rural routes.** HARRY HAY

Right **Although broadly similar to 40 Tiger Cubs supplied to Alexander's in 1954, this vehicle was an oddity in the Midland fleet. It was one of two early Alexander-bodied Tiger Cub demonstrators – it had a 1952-series chassis number – that had been purchased in 1954 by Glasgow independent Lowland Motorways. The Lowland business was acquired in 1958 by Scottish Omnibuses, where the Tiger Cub was a non-standard type, and consequently both vehicles were transferred to Alexander's in exchange for a pair of AEC Monocoaches of similar vintage. They were sold by Midland in 1970. The location for this view is Germiston Street, where vehicles could be seen on layover outside Glasgow's Buchanan Street bus station.** HARRY HAY

Below **This style of Alexander body was supplied to Alexander's on 60 Tiger Cubs and 99 Reliances and Monocoaches in the period 1954-7. The Tiger Cubs were in the Southern and Fife Areas, the Reliances in the Southern and Northern Areas. Northern initially painted them in coach livery, although most were 45-seat buses. Both Fife and Midland treated all vehicles with this style of body as buses, and repainted them accordingly. This 41-seat Reliance is seen at Northern's Aberdeen depot.** HARRY HAY

Not only had SBG adopted a cautious approach to rear-engined double-deckers, it was equally wary of the new generation of low-frame rear-engined single-deckers, with some justification. Fife's interest in AECs had prompted it to test a rear-engined Swift demonstrator, with Willowbrook bus body, in Kirkcaldy in 1966, but no orders resulted. However, an unusual purchase by the company in 1969 was of a batch of 12 Bristol RELL6Gs with 53-seat ECW bus bodies. Despite being quite different from any other vehicles in the fleet, the REs were not concentrated at any one depot or on any specific routes, although they did appear regularly on services to Edinburgh. The only other 53-seat buses with Fife at this time were six AEC Reliances dating from 1964.

Midland's 1969 Leopards, while outwardly similar to previous deliveries, were based on PSU3A/4R chassis with Pneumocyclic gearboxes. There were eight. Subsequent deliveries would revert to the PSU3/3R, with four-speed manual gearboxes – at least until 1977. Northern had six Leopards on order for 1969, but these were diverted to Scottish Omnibuses, which sent six of its troublesome 1966 AEC Reliances to Aberdeen. The 590-engined Reliances overheated when driven hard; they were expected to lead less strenuous lives with Northern. Northern lagged behind the other Alexander's companies in adopting 36ft-long vehicles. In 1969 it had just 22 – the six ex-Scottish Omnibuses Reliances and 16 Leopards. By contrast, Fife had 38 – the 12 RELLs plus 26 Reliances – while Midland had 90, all Leopards.

One-man-operation was a contentious subject in the late 1960s, provoking strong opposition from the Transport & General Workers' Union in many areas. The union was concerned about the loss of conductors' jobs. But by the end of the decade, it was clear that driver-only-operation was the future, and all three Alexander's companies were running small numbers of one-man buses on rural routes. Midland had set the ball rolling in the early 1960s when it converted a solitary Leyland Tiger for use as a one-man bus for operation at Pitlochry depot, and this was soon followed by Albion Nimbuses at Crieff. Drivers of one-man buses were paid a premium for doing the job of collecting fares – 15% over the basic hourly rate on a single-decker, 20% on a double-decker. In addition, both drivers and remaining conductors at

Above **Northern inherited 20 Leyland PD3s, all with 67-seat lowbridge Alexander bodies. One of the first to be repainted yellow had its livery applied in the same style as had been used for the previous blue. This was clearly deemed to be not quite right, and a number of other layouts were tried before settling on the use of cream for the lower-deck window surrounds. This view is in Union Street, Aberdeen, with a Reliance in Bluebird coach livery behind the Titan, and an Aberdeen Corporation Daimler CVG6 heading in the opposite direction.**
STEWART J. BROWN COLLECTION

each depot were paid a bonus calculated on the cost savings achieved by reducing the number of conductors at the depot.

A programme of equipping vehicles for driver-only-operation was started by all three companies from 1967. This typically involved providing a suitable warning on the front (usually a hinged plate or an illuminated sign below the nearside windscreen), installing a cradle to hold the Setright ticket machine, along with a coin tray, and fitting a reversing light. The approval of the Traffic Commissioner was required for routes on which vehicles had to reverse at a terminus, and this could involve revising routes to eliminate the need for the driver of a one-man bus to reverse without the assistance of a conductor. Surprisingly there was no increase in running times for services converted to driver-only-operation, even on busy routes running into Glasgow.

In 1968, Fife recorded just 21 buses in its fleet as having been converted – 20 Tiger Cubs and the solitary Bedford VAS bus. By 1971, the conversion programme had gained momentum, and new vehicles were being delivered already equipped for one-man-operation; in that year Midland had 275 OMO-fitted buses, including 75 double-deckers. And by 1975, in all three fleets, virtually every bus that could be converted had been. The oldest conversions, apart from Midland's early Tiger, were mid-1950s Reliances and Tiger Cubs.

The idea of trying to match registration numbers with fleet numbers was one which the Alexander's companies adopted from the mid-1960s. Previously the companies

had typically booked a single block of consecutive numbers to cover each year's planned intake of new buses – for example, in 1962 the 36 new buses for Fife were registered 7401-36 SP, which series covered Lodekkas, Lowlanders, Reliances and Bedford VASs. Fife first used matching fleet and registration numbers on new AEC Reliances in 1963, seemed to forget about the idea in 1964, but then, along with Northern, switched to trying to match registration numbers with fleet numbers from 1965; Midland did not follow suit until 1970.

At the end of the 1960s the three Alexander's fleets were changing rapidly. The biggest sign of change was the ubiquitous Y-type; by the end of 1969 the three companies between them had almost 450 examples – 201 at Midland, 145 at Northern and 95 at Fife. Rear-engined double-deckers, meanwhile, had arrived at Fife and Midland, which between them were running 90 Alexander-bodied Fleetlines. And older types were continuing to disappear. The last of Fife's austere Guy Arab IIs had gone in 1968, by which time they were a remarkable 24 years old. The last Arab III single-deckers left the Fife fleet in the same year, mere youngsters at 20. Fife's last Leyland Tiger PS1s were withdrawn in 1969, and its last half-cab single-deckers, OPS2 Tigers, followed in 1970. The unrebuilt OPS2s, which had retained their O.600 engines, were withdrawn at the same time as the last of those that had been rebuilt to PS1 standard. Similarly Midland's last half-cab single-deckers, PS1s and OPS2s, were withdrawn in 1970, along with the last of its Regent IIIs. The last PD1s had left the fleet in 1968.

Right **An attractive new Alexander dual-purpose body, normally fitted with 41 seats, was supplied to Alexander's from 1958, the last being delivered to the new Fife company in 1961. This style was fitted to three different chassis – AEC Reliance, Leyland Tiger Cub and Albion Aberdonian – and there were detail differences between each year's production. Here a 1958 Northern Aberdonian unloads in Glasgow, having arrived from Dundee on the limited-stop service. Reflecting the popularity of the James Bond films in the early 1960s, it claims to be on route 007 rather than on the 21, which was the correct number. Note the lady and gentleman who are going to collect their luggage from the boot are both wearing hats – no doubt the height of style for the well-dressed 1960s coach passenger.** HARRY HAY

Right **Looking uncharacteristically tired, a 1959 Midland Tiger Cub lays over in Falkirk bus station in 1968. Detail differences from the 1958 Aberdonian include a deeper grille, rectangular side lights – the shape of these changed from year to year – and a fixed driver's windscreen. Midland operated two routes between Falkirk and Airdrie. This Tiger Cub will be going via Slamannan, a 50-minute journey; the alternative route served Allandale and Cumbernauld and took an hour.** HARRY HAY

Left Reliances of this style were in both the Midland and Northern fleets. This is a 1960 coach, with revised grille, no bumper and no 'V' below the windscreen. The short centre bay housed the emergency exit. This Macduff-based coach is seen in Aberdeen bus station, having arrived on the lengthy service from Inverness via the coast. Whereas Midland and Fife would repaint bodies of this style as buses as the vehicles aged, in the Northern fleet they retained coach livery throughout their lives.
HARRY HAY

Left The final bodies of this style, taking the total to 212 on three different chassis types, were delivered to the new Fife company in 1961. These Tiger Cubs originally wore Alexander's cream-and-blue coach livery, were then repainted in Fife coach livery and finally adopted Fife bus livery, as did other vehicles with this style of body. Alongside at Fife's St Andrews depot stands a Tiger OPS2 with 35-seat Alexander body, still regarded as a coach despite its obsolete design and advancing years. The Tiger Cub has been equipped for one-man-operation and carries a flap above the nearside headlamp to indicate this. The hinged flap could be closed when there was a conductor on board. The OPS2 is one of three that retained their original O.600 engines. It survived until 1970, by which time it was 20 years old; the Tiger Cub had a 16-year life with Fife.
HARRY HAY

Right **The first new coaches for Midland were 19 Tiger Cubs with a new style of Alexander body, seating 38 passengers. The body used the same structure as on previous deliveries but with new glass fibre front and rear panels, new side mouldings, glazed cove panels and, a briefly fashionable feature, twin headlights. They were attractive coaches but remained unique, as a fire at the Alexander factory destroyed the glass fibre moulds. In any event they would soon be eclipsed by an all-new coach body from Alexander. This Tiger Cub is operating a tour on behalf of Thomas Cook in Aberdeen in 1965. The tiny notice at the top corner of the nearside windscreen reads 'On hire to Thos Cook & Son' – a reminder that in the days when tours had to be licensed by the Traffic Commissioner the licence for this tour was held by Thomas Cook and not by Midland.**
HARRY HAY

Right **In 1961, Alexander's took delivery of 17 buses which used new PD3 chassis frames supplied by Leyland, into which were fitted engines, gearboxes and axles transferred from 10-year-old Tiger OPS2s. They had standard Alexander 67-seat lowbridge bodies but were immediately identifiable by their exposed radiators. All passed to Midland. This gleaming example in Glasgow shows the improved livery adopted by Midland, with three bands of cream relief – originally there had been just one, below the lower-deck windows – complete with lining out. The fleetname harks back to the pre-1961 Alexander style and was used only from 1965 to 1968.** HARRY HAY

Left **The 1962 coaches for all three companies had this style of Alexander body, on Reliance chassis for Fife and Northern and on Tiger Cubs for Midland. It had originally been developed for the BET group. This is a Tiger Cub, preparing to depart Glasgow's Dundas Street bus station on a tour to Oban and Land of Lorne, according to a clear plastic board just visible in the windscreen. Although there were only 49 bodies of this style, all delivered in 1962, there were numerous variations.** HARRY HAY

Left **Most of the 1962 BET-style bodies were equipped as coaches, but 10 of those for Northern were 45-seat buses, albeit with high-backed seats, in the Alexander's tradition of running what were often described as dual-purpose vehicles. This offered sufficient comfort for them to be used on tours, as apparent from this view of an Aberdeen-based bus in Elgin when new.** ALISTAIR DOUGLAS

Right **Midland tried a brighter livery style on just four double-deckers in 1963. They included this Leyland PD3A, one of a batch of 18 which had in 1961 been the company's first new double-deckers. These and six similar buses supplied to Northern were the last new Titans for either company. This one is arriving in Glasgow on the service from Falkirk via Kilsyth, a journey which took around 1 hour 20 minutes, depending on precisely which route was taken – there were four variations.** HARRY HAY

Right **Fife received seven new Lowlanders with Alexander bodies, delivered alongside further examples of the Bristol Lodekka, which had been the standard Fife Area double-decker since 1956. They were allocated to the busy service between Dunfermline, Cowdenbeath and Ballingry, which ran every 10 minutes from 7am to 11pm on weekdays and every six minutes from 9am to 11pm on Saturdays, with marginally less frequent operation at other times. This is the turning area at the back of Dunfermline's main bus station in Carnegie Street; there was also a smaller terminus in St Margaret Street, used by services that left the town by way of Rosyth.** HARRY HAY

Left **Only seven new Lowlanders were bought by Fife, but the company soon began receiving second-hand examples from Central SMT and Western SMT. Fife's paint shop could not immediately cope with this influx of buses – 18 from Central in 1965 alone – so the Lowlanders were placed in service in their previous owners' liveries, as demonstrated by a former Central bus, with Northern Counties body, leaving Dunfermline bus station for Ballingry. By 1967, there would be 39 Lowlanders in the Fife fleet.** HARRY HAY

Left **Each of the Alexander's companies received a Bedford VAS, with a Duple Midland bus body, in 1962. All three were delivered in blue, those for Fife and Northern being the last vehicles supplied in that colour. This is Fife's bus, which was based initially at Newburgh and was soon repainted red. Newburgh was one of Fife's smallest depots, with an allocation of 13 vehicles, all single-deckers.**
STEWART J. BROWN COLLECTION

Above **Northern took Y-type Reliances, 40 in all, in 1963 and 1964. In this 1972 view one of the 1964 coaches is heading out of Portgordon on the Aberdeen-Inverness service, with the Moray Firth in the background. It displays the revised fleetname adopted in 1971. Most vehicles on the coast route to Inverness did not make the entire five-and-a-half-hour trip – indeed, there were just three through trips a day, through passengers being encouraged to use the direct route via Huntly, which took one hour less, even with a change of bus at Elgin. The black smoke from the exhaust was untypical.**
STEWART J. BROWN

Right **Unique in the Midland fleet was this Albion Viking VK41L demonstrator, which was based at the company's Perth depot for six months in the winter of 1964/5, after having been an exhibit at the 1963 Scottish Motor Show. It is seen sweeping out of Tay Street, Perth, on the service to Dundee. Its Alexander Y-type body had 41 bus seats The VK41L had a front-mounted engine.** HARRY HAY

Left Midland's first Alexander Y-types, in 1963, comprised 22 on Leyland Tiger Cub chassis and five on AEC Reliance; similar coaches on Reliance chassis were delivered to Fife and Northern. The last six of Midland's 1963 Tiger Cubs were specified as touring coaches with public-address systems and an illuminated fleetname panel – the only coaches in the fleet with this feature. One is seen on a private hire in Dunoon. The block Midland name on the front dates this as a post-1965 view. HARRY HAY

Left In 1965 Northern acquired the business of Strachan's of Ballater, retaining the company's two most modern vehicles. This Duple-bodied Reliance was 11 years old when acquired by Northern and had been new to Wallace Arnold of Leeds. Seen in Aberdeen depot in 1966, it survived until 1973, by which time it was 19 years old. HARRY HAY

Right **The 53-seat bus-style Y-type would come to typify Scottish Bus Group vehicles for much of the 1960s and '70s, and all three Alexander's companies were early users of the type. Midland took its first, on Leyland Leopard chassis, in 1964. Fife took similar buses, but on Reliance chassis, in the same year. At Northern the 53-seat Leopard was later in arriving, the first entering service in 1968; there were six, and Northern, like Midland, painted them in coach livery. Here one loads in Aberdeen bus station for Rosehearty when new. Y-type buses lacked the chrome bumper of coach models.** HARRY HAY

Right **In 1966, Midland took over the 30-vehicle business of Carmichael of Glenboig. Among the newer vehicles in the fleet were four Willowbrook-bodied Leyland Leopards, one of which is seen pausing at Carmichael's Greenfoot garage on its way from Moodiesburn to Coatbridge, one of the company's main routes. It displays its Midland fleet number above the offside headlamp, along with an allocation plate for the new Cumbernauld depot which replaced Carmichael's premises in 1968.** HARRY HAY

Above **Fife was the last of the Alexander's companies to buy new rear-entrance double-deckers, taking 34 FS6G Lodekkas in 1963 and 1964. A 1964 bus stands in Kirkcaldy's town service bus station in 1972. It has a Kirkcaldy XA registration, Kirkcaldy having become a vehicle-licensing authority in 1963. All new Fife buses would have Kirkcaldy registrations until 1974; thereafter they would be registered in Edinburgh, following an overhaul of the vehicle licensing system.**
STEWART J. BROWN

Left **Albion Vikings with rear-mounted engines – the VK43 range – were bought by all three Alexander's companies. All had Y-type bodies, most with 40 seats. Midland built up a fleet of 75, represented here by a 1967 coach in Falkirk bus station.**
HARRY HAY

Right **Among the 15 Carmichael vehicles to receive Midland livery were five 1957 Leyland Royal Tiger Worldmasters, which had been new to Glasgow Corporation Transport but were mechanically similar to the Royal Tigers in the Midland fleet. Note the use of the route-number box to display the Highland fleetname that had been used by Carmichael. The 44-seat bodywork was built by Glasgow Corporation on Weymann frames. These buses would be withdrawn in 1970/1.** HARRY HAY

Right **Burnett of Mintlaw operated 14 AECs when the business was purchased by Northern. One of the more exotic examples was this Reliance with 34-seat Harrington body, which had been new in 1955 to McIntyre of Bucksburn – one of Harrington's few Scottish customers. Note Northern's fleet number above the offside headlamp in this photograph, taken in Mintlaw.** HARRY HAY

Left **Nine of Burnett's vehicles received Northern livery, among them this Reliance with Burlingham Seagull bodywork, which had been new to Burnett in 1957. The design of the entrance door is particularly neat, with glazing and mouldings that appear to continue unbroken along the side of the coach. This vehicle was to serve Northern until 1973.** HARRY HAY

Left **Over the years Alexander's and its successors operated a number of ex-London Transport buses but only one RT-class AEC Regent, which came with the Simpson's business at the end of 1966. The 1947 Park Royal-bodied bus is seen in Northern ownership – the tell-tale fleet number is below the offside side lamp – operating on the ex-Simpson Fraserburgh town service. It would be withdrawn in 1968 without being repainted.** HARRY HAY

Above **The opening of the Tay Road Bridge in 1966 provided new opportunities to create links between Fife and Dundee. Fife diverted a number of routes, which had previously served the southern terminal of the cross-river ferry at Tayport, to run direct to Dundee. This 1962 FLF Lodekka heading north across the bridge is on the service from Leven. A Fife Tiger Cub can be seen in the distance on the bridge, which is carrying remarkably little traffic in this July 1973 view. The bridge is 1.4 miles long and cost £5 million to build.** STEWART J. BROWN

Right **Although it operated 45 Leyland Tiger PS1s, Fife had no Titan PD1s – until the arrival of this bus from Western SMT in 1967. The chassis had been new in 1949, the 53-seat ECW body in 1952. While it should have carried an FRA-series fleet number (in line with established Alexander's practice), it was instead numbered as an FRB – the series for PD2 and PD3 Titans with O.600 engines. It remained Fife's only PD1 and was operated for three years.**

HARRY HAY

Left Among the strangest vehicles acquired by Northern from the independents it took over were three Bristol LWL6Bs that came with the business of Mitchell of Luthermuir in October 1967. They had ECW bodies and were the only Bristol-engined vehicles to be operated by an Alexander's company. This coach had been new in 1951 to the Southern National Omnibus Co. Despite being completely non-standard it survived for three years with Northern, albeit retaining Mitchell's livery; in this view the only signs of Northern's ownership are the legal lettering on the door and a near-invisible disc with the fleet number, located at the bottom of the driver's windscreen. HARRY HAY

Left The newer vehicles in the Mitchell fleet were repainted, and these included four Fords. This 1961 Plaxton Embassy-bodied 570E had started life with Garelochhead Coach Services and is seen parked outside Northern's Montrose depot in 1968. HARRY HAY

Right **Unusual in Scotland were 12 Bristol RELL6Gs with 53-seat ECW bodies, delivered to Fife in 1968. They were often to be found on services running to Edinburgh, the location for this 1977 view of a bus on the service from Glenrothes.** MARK BAILEY

Right **The last big Bedford coaches for Midland were 15 VAMs with 45-seat Duple Viceroy bodies, delivered in 1967. They introduced a new Midland Bluebird fleetname, which would be applied to all subsequent Duple-bodied coaches until 1978. This coach is seen on a private hire in George Square, Glasgow, in 1975. The VAMs were withdrawn in 1977.**

STEWART J. BROWN

Above **New Alexander-bodied Daimler Fleetlines appeared in the Midland fleet in 1967 and with Fife in 1968. They were the first rear-engined double-deckers for either company. Alexander built the stylish low-height 75-seat bodywork. A smart Fife example is seen on a Dunfermline town service, passing under the railway line which heads south to the Forth Bridge.** STEWART J. BROWN

Left **Parked at Edinburgh's Turnhouse Airport in 1967 is one of the most exotic vehicles to run for Northern – an Austin Princess Vanden Plas seven-seat limousine. The roof-mounted board, which seems out of keeping with the car's stately appearance, promotes the service that connected Dundee with British United Airways flights to London. A discreet disc on the windscreen carries the fleet number, NX1.** STEWART J. BROWN

Consolidation and Rationalisation

Above **Midland's last new
Bedfords, in 1970, were seven
VAS5s with Duple Vista 25
bodies. They were used
primarily on Highland tours,
on which many roads were
still unsuitable for large
coaches. Here one of the little
Bedfords is guided off the
ferry from Skye at Kyle of
Lochalsh in 1972. Note the
white-topped driver's hat
lodged on the dashboard; the
elasticated white cover was
a feature of tour drivers' hats
and could be removed when
the driver was on routine
service duties.** STEWART J. BROWN

THERE WAS NO LACK OF variety in the three Alexander's
fleets in the 1960s, but the 1970s would prove to be a
decade of rationalisation. AEC had disappeared from the
companies' orders after Fife's 1966 delivery. Albion was
the next supplier to disappear, the last Vikings entering
service at Northern in 1970. Although purists could
reasonably argue that Lowlanders were not 'real' Albions,
if you count Lowlanders, Aberdonians, and Vikings, the
marque had enjoyed something of a renaissance in the
Alexander's fleets, and in 1970 there were around 320 in
operation throughout the three companies.

Bedford, which had been a supplier of coaches from
Alexander's early days, was also delivering its last coaches
in 1970, in the form of seven VASs for Midland and four
VAMs for Northern, all bodied by Duple.

And Bristol's future as a supplier was looking bleak. In
the 1960s, Fife and Midland had between them bought 107
Lodekkas, these joining 152 inherited from the pre-1961
Alexander's company. In 1970, having bought only Fleetlines
since 1967, Midland divided its double-deck order between
Daimler and Bristol, taking 15 VRTs with Gardner engines
and ECW 77-seat bodies. They operated in the Falkirk and
Stirling areas, the first entering service in February 1970.

Such was their performance that by October 1971, all 15
had been sold to Eastern National, Midland taking 15 five-
year-old FLF Lodekkas in part exchange. It was a damning
indictment of the VRT and marked the end of Bristol as a
supplier of double-deckers. The Eastern National Lodekkas
were, incidentally, the only second-hand vehicles from
outside SBG to be purchased by Midland.

Bristol briefly fared better with single-deckers. After
abandoning the Viking, Midland switched its allegiance to
the Bristol LH6P with Perkins engine and, of course,
Alexander Y-type body. Considering that the LH was
available with Leyland's familiar 6.54-litre O.400 engine,
the choice of the smaller Perkins H6.354 5.8-litre unit
was surprising. To provide an adequate airflow for the
LH's front-mounted radiator the body had a different
front panel from that used on Midland's existing Y-types.
The company's first LHs, in 1970, were eight 38-seat
touring coaches, followed by eleven 41-seaters. Further
LHs followed in 1971 and 1972, giving Midland a total of
41. The last three were 45-seat buses with short windows
and were the first Midland Y-types to be delivered in blue
bus livery. These were also Midland's last Bristols. Neither
Fife nor Northern tried the LH.

Left **In the period 1970-2, Midland took 41 Bristol LHs – all with Alexander Y-type bodies and most of them 41-seaters, like this 1971 coach in Dundas Street bus station in 1975. The LHs were immediately identifiable by the large front grille, necessary to provide adequate airflow to the front-mounted radiator. Although constituting a relatively small class, the LHs could be found at depots throughout Midland's territory.**
IAIN MACGREGOR

By the spring of 1970, Midland was running 85 Fleetlines with stylish Alexander bodies, but later that year it would take a dozen that were bodied by ECW. The ECW body, with its flat-glass windscreens, lacked the flair of the Alexander product. Fourteen similar buses were delivered to Fife in 1971, along with an odd batch of five bodied by Northern Counties – the first new bodies to be delivered from the Wigan builder to an Alexander's company since a solitary Guy Arab (which had been ordered by Greig of Inverness) in 1947. The bodies were part of an order cancelled by Western SMT.

Three single-deck demonstrators were evaluated by Midland in 1970 – a Bedford YRQ, a Daimler Fleetline SRG6 and a Metro-Scania. The two high-capacity rear-engined buses were operated from Larbert on a Falkirk local service, normally worked by Lodekkas or Fleetlines, and on the Falkirk-Alloa service. The YRQ, which had a Duple Viceroy coach body, was used on the Callander-Edinburgh service, running alongside Leyland Leopards.

From 1970, SBG started absorbing the bus and coach operations of David MacBrayne. Most affected by this was Highland Omnibuses, which took over the bulk of the MacBrayne business. However, MacBrayne's established holiday-tours operation, based in Glasgow, was taken over by Midland and ultimately amalgamated with Midland's own programme of extended tours. As part of the deal Midland acquired 18 Duple-bodied Bedford VAS coaches from MacBrayne in the autumn of 1970. Four were sold without being used, and the remainder were repainted in Midland livery, even though five were used only for the 1971 summer season before being sold to Glasgow-based Bedford dealer SMT Sales & Service. The well-maintained

six-year-old coaches soon found appreciative buyers. MacBrayne specified simpler side mouldings on its Duple bodies in place of Duple's standard style, and the coaches acquired by Midland were initially painted in a simple livery of blue below the waist and cream above. The effect was rather sombre, and a cream skirt was soon added.

One other effect of the integration of MacBrayne's business with that of Highland Omnibuses was a redrawing of Highland's territory to include Midland's Oban depot. This was transferred to Highland in October 1970, along with the 14 vehicles based there. These

Below **Northern was the biggest operator of the Viking VK43L, buying 88 new between 1965 and 1970 and then adding six ex-Eastern Scottish coaches in 1972. This one is seen in Elgin in 1976 on the service which ran between Burghead and New Elgin. By this time all of Northern's buses were equipped for driver-only-operation. Almost-invisible red lettering on the lower edge of the nearside windscreen advises passengers to 'Pay as you enter'.** STEWART J. BROWN

Above **A dreary winter's day in Falkirk bus station, with a 1970 Midland Fleetline showing the revised front panel used by Alexander on deliveries between 1970 and 1976. This bus is equipped for one-man-operation, as indicated by the sign on the front, above the Midland fleetname. A board above the platform advises passengers which services depart from the stance, including those to Grangemouth via the quaintly named Fouldubs.** STEWART J. BROWN

Right **Also delivered in 1970 were Midland's first ECW-bodied Fleetlines. There were 12, eight of which would be transferred to Northern in 1977, including this bus seen on a Perth city service in the summer of that year.** STEWART J. BROWN

included nine Leyland Tiger Cubs, a type not hitherto operated by Highland; they were quickly exchanged for a like number of AEC Reliances of similar vintage. The Oban-Glasgow service became a joint operation between Midland, from Stepps depot, and Highland.

Northern's limousine service between Dundee and Edinburgh Airport was expanded with additional vehicles – two seven-seat Ford Dorchesters in 1970 (one of which replaced the original Princess), followed by another two in

1971/2. The Dorchester was a lengthened version of the Zodiac Mk IV saloon, the conversion work being carried out by specialist builder Coleman Milne of Bolton. In 1973, demand for the service had grown to the point where a 1968 Bedford VAS coach was down-seated to 16 and painted in British Caledonian livery, to be followed in 1974 by a second VAS, which received British Airways colours. British Caledonian was the successor to British United, the airline originally associated with the limousine

Left **Less successful 1970 deliveries were Midland's 15 Bristol VRTs. They left the fleet in 1971, heading south to Eastern National in exchange for a like number of Bristol Lodekkas. Here a Bannockburn-based bus heads through Stirling on the cross-town service from Cornton.** IAIN MACGREGOR

service. Two of the Ford limousines were withdrawn in 1973; the remaining two were sold in 1975. The switch from limousines to coaches made economic sense, no doubt, but the travel experience was rather different, changing from the quiet luxury of a V6 petrol-engined limousine to a noisy diesel-powered truck-derived coach.

Having had no double-deckers join the fleet since the two Lowlanders in 1963, Northern in 1970 started replacing Titans delivered in the late 1940s and early 1950s with marginally younger vehicles transferred from Western SMT. To describe the process as modernisation would be stretching a point, as the buses heading north were typically 14 years old. But, however you look at it, 31 PD2s, with bodywork by Northern Counties or Alexander, joined the Northern fleet in 1970/1. As they arrived, out went 23-year-old PD1s and 20-year-old PD2s. The ousted vehicles included the last ex-Sutherland buses, a dozen PD1s and two AEC Regent IIIs.

Unusual acquisitions at Northern in 1970 were two 1958 Plaxton-bodied AEC Reliances that had been new to prominent English coach operators Sheffield United Tours and Wallace Arnold and had latterly been operated by Carson of Dunvegan, whose business was acquired by MacBrayne in February 1970. They passed to Highland Omnibuses, where they were not used, in May and thence to Northern in September. The ex-Wallace Arnold coach, which had a centre-entrance body, was not used in service and instead was converted to a training vehicle; the former SUT vehicle, rebuilt with power-operated jack-knife doors and fitted with a roof-mounted destination display, ran with Northern until 1976.

In 1971, Northern abandoned the script fleetname introduced in 1962, replacing it with a new underlined

lower-case fleetname in black, outlined in white. The style was similar to that used by Midland. Some vehicles also bore the company's name in block letters on the front.

Both Midland and Northern had been running 36ft Leopards since 1965. At the start of 1970, Midland had 90, and Northern 16, including six coach-liveried 53-seat buses delivered in 1969. Fife, which had followed its batches of 36ft Reliances with an order for Bristol RELLs, finally switched to Leopards in 1970, taking 13 with standard 49-seat Y-type bodies. More would follow in 1972/3, quickly taking its fleet to 50. Fife also expanded its Fleetline fleet, adding 52 in 1970/1. These included the 14 with ECW bodies and the five bodied by Northern Counties. A further two chassis intended for 1971 delivery were cancelled and taken up by McGill's of Barrhead.

Below **Seen in Glasgow in 1974, an ex-MacBrayne Bedford VAS unloads passengers returning from a holiday tour. Midland retained 14 of the VASs it acquired from MacBrayne in 1970. MacBrayne used simplified side mouldings on its Duple Bella Vista bodies, and these coaches were originally all-blue below the windows, which looked drab; the cream skirt was added to improve their appearance.** STEWART J. BROWN

Right **Fife was the last of the Alexander's companies to embrace the 36ft Leopard, receiving its first examples in 1970. By 1974 it would be running 50 Y-type Leopards of this style, after which it added a further 95 with short-windowed bus bodies. Although equipped for one-man-operation, this coach was crew-operated when photographed in 1976 on the half-hourly service from Dunfermline to North Queensferry.** STEWART J. BROWN

The quest for a light-duty bus for rural services had not been abandoned. At the start of the 1970s, Northern was withdrawing its last Leyland Tigers, typically 21 or 22 years old, and in 1972 it would start taking early underfloor-engined vehicles out of service, beginning with its 16 Royal Tigers and 10 Tiger Cubs. These would be followed from 1973 by early AEC Reliances and Monocoaches. The model chosen to replace these was the Ford R-series, starting in 1971 with fifteen 36ft-long R226s with 53-seat short-windowed Y-type bus bodies. To the casual observer a Y-type Leopard and a Y-type Ford looked much the same, but, once you were on board, the Ford's front-mounted engine signalled that this was going to be a rather less sophisticated travel experience than riding on a Leopard. A Ford was about a ton lighter than a Leopard and had a much smaller engine – a 5.96-litre unit compared with the Leopard's 9.8 litres.

The Ford engine was turbocharged and despite its size was rated at 150bhp, which was actually 20bhp more than a Leopard, although from 1972, SBG Leopards would feature the bigger 11.1-litre 680, rated at 155bhp.

More Fords quickly followed, and by the end of 1974 Northern had bought 80 new R-series. Most were bodied by Alexander, and there were short 41-seat coaches and 45-seat buses and long 49-seat coaches and 53-seat buses. Whatever the seating configuration, they were all delivered in coach livery. There were also half a dozen coaches with 45-seat Duple Dominant bodies, which were delivered in 1974. In its 1975 Annual Report the Scottish Bus Group commented favourably on its experience running Fords, stating – without mentioning Ford by name – that 'Particular success has been achieved in the operation and economy of light-weight vehicles.' What it didn't say – because it didn't yet know – was that there would be issues concerning durability.

Midland, which had bought Duple-bodied Bedford VAM coaches in 1967, also introduced Duple-bodied Ford coaches to its fleet in 1974, taking ten 41-seaters. In addition, it took ten 53-seat Ford/Alexander buses, but, unlike Northern, it also continued buying Leopard buses for busier routes. More Fords, both Duple-bodied coaches and Alexander-bodied buses, were delivered in 1975. Midland stopped buying Fords in 1978, by which time it had 69 – 32 Duple coaches and 37 Y-type buses.

Fife also tried Fords, taking ten R1014s with 45-seat Duple Dominant coach bodies in 1974 and seven R1114s with 53-seat Alexander bus bodies in 1975. The Fords had relatively short lives with Fife. The coaches were transferred to Northern and Highland in 1979; the buses passed to Highland in 1982. A further four Duple coaches, ordered for 1976, were diverted to Highland before delivery.

Below **Duple revamped the Viceroy body in 1968, and the result was a much sharper-looking coach than the original. Northern had six of the new-look Viceroys – four Bedford VAMs in 1970, followed by two Ford R1014s in 1972. This is one of the Fords, seen in Blackpool in the summer of 1978. They operated for 10 years with Northern.** MARK BAILEY

Above **The idea behind buying Fords for Northern was that they would help cut costs on rural services. That they would also be used on more demanding inter-urban services, as demonstrated here by a coach on the 85-mile route from Dundee to Glasgow, was not part of the original plan. This is a 1973 R1014, with 41 coach seats in its Alexander body, on the main A9 road near Cairnie's Brae, north of Aberuthven, in April 1977.** STEWART J. BROWN

Left **Northern modernised its double-deck fleet in 1970/1 by acquiring 31 Leyland Titan PD2s from Western SMT. Two 1957 Northern Counties-bodied PD2s are seen at Elgin depot in 1972. The ex-Western PD2s typically ran with Northern for five years.** STEWART J. BROWN

Right **All three Alexander's companies bought new Fords in the mid-1970s. Those at Fife had the shortest lives with their original owner. Ten R1014s with 45-seat Duple Dominant bodywork were purchased in 1974/5, and in 1979 they were transferred out of the fleet, being shared equally between Northern and Highland. One is seen in Blackpool in July 1979, towards the end of its time with Fife, running on hire to Central SMT.** MARK BAILEY

Right **In 1974, Midland took over the service between Aberfeldy and Pitlochry operated by Aberfeldy Motor Coaches, and with it two Bedford YRQs with differing styles of Willowbrook bodywork. The newer of the two had a 49-seat bus body, as seen here in Perth bus station in 1977; the other was a coach with a panoramic-windowed Expressway body. Both were allocated to Crieff depot.** MARK BAILEY

In 1969, the Government had introduced a New Bus Grant scheme, whereby it would contribute 25% (later increased to 50%) of the purchase price of new vehicles that were suitable for one-man-operation. This funding was available for vehicles to coach specification as long as they had features such as power-operated doors and destination screens and covered at least 50% of their annual mileage on stage-carriage services (the term then in use to describe regular scheduled local bus routes). The

Duple-bodied coaches delivered to the three Alexander's companies in the 1970s were to this specification and could thus be used on tours in the summer, then fitted with ticket machines for winter use as one-man buses.

There were a few vehicle transfers between SBG fleets in the mid-1970s. In 1974, Northern acquired, from Scottish Omnibuses, the only AEC Regent Vs operated by the Group – two Massey-bodied buses that had been new in 1957 to Baxter's of Airdrie. They were operated for just

six months, mainly on school services in Dundee, and were not repainted. At around the same time Northern acquired two Bedford VAS coaches from Midland. One operated briefly in Northern colours before being repainted in British Airways livery – for the Edinburgh Airport service – to replace a coach destroyed by fire.

There was one small takeover by Midland in 1974, of Aberfeldy Motor Coaches. The company ran a service to Pitlochry and owned two Willowbrook-bodied Bedford YRQs. Although a non-standard type in the Midland fleet, both vehicles, which were two years old, were taken into stock and allocated to Crieff depot. They were operated until 1982.

Rarely the recipient of vehicles transferred from other group companies, Midland in 1975 received no fewer than 24 – its first since a deal with Scottish Omnibuses in 1963 which saw Midland acquire a solitary ex-Baxter's Tiger Cub (non-standard in the Scottish Omnibuses fleet) in exchange for an AEC Reliance. First came nine ECW-bodied Fleetlines from Central SMT. These were four years old, and in exchange Midland supplied Central with a like number of 53-seat Leopard buses of broadly similar vintage. This exchange was driven by Central's desire to be rid of its Fleetlines. From Fife came that company's unique batch of five Fleetlines with Northern Counties bodies. These too were four years old. Finally, from Scottish Omnibuses, came ten 49-seat Leopards, which were just 12 months old.

In the first half of the 1970s the Midland fleet shrank dramatically, not so much from service cutbacks – although these were having an effect – but rather through more efficient scheduling and the introduction of bigger buses. Single-deckers leaving the fleet at the start of the 1970s

were either 35- or 41-seaters; their replacements were in the main 49- and 53-seaters. Departing double-deckers were 53-seaters; new arrivals seated 75. In the six years from 1970 to 1975 there was a net reduction of almost 200 vehicles, or 20%. However, there were no depot closures – not until 1983, when Stirling depot closed, and its operations were transferred to nearby Bannockburn. A look at the allocations of these two depots is illustrative of the scale of the reductions being made across the fleet. In the mid-1960s Stirling had an allocation of 84 vehicles, while Bannockburn had 57. A decade later the two depots between them had just 93 buses – little more than Stirling's allocation 10 years earlier.

The opening of new stretches of motorway and high-grade dual-carriageway provided new opportunities for long-distance coach services, in particular from Aberdeen

and Glenrothes to London, with intermediate pick-ups on the way. In 1974/5, Northern borrowed London-specification Bristol RE coaches from Western SMT and Scottish Omnibuses, for use on the new Aberdeen-London service, before taking delivery of its own London coaches – six Leyland Leopard PSU5s with Alexander's distinctive high-floor M-type body. These were the company's first 12m-long coaches and had 42 reclining seats, double-glazing, an auxiliary oil-fired heater and a rear toilet compartment.

Fife, similarly, had borrowed Bristol REs from Scottish Omnibuses in 1974 for its Glenrothes-London service and in 1975 took four PSU5s with M-type bodies. Three were new; the fourth was a six-month-old coach transferred from Scottish Omnibuses. Two similar Scottish Omnibuses coaches joined the Northern fleet towards the end of 1975. Both Fife's and Northern's London coaches were

operated briefly in company livery, but in 1976 a new Group-wide corporate identity, blue and white with the fleetname 'Scottish', was adopted for all London services and was applied to Fife's and Northern's M-type Leopards. Northern promoted its service as 'The Northern Scot'. It is a measure of the Leopard's durability that one of Northern's PSU5s would cover 750,000 miles without needing an engine overhaul. The Fife service to London originally went via the Forth Road Bridge and Edinburgh, but in 1977 was re-routed to provide connections to London from Falkirk and Cumbernauld.

Also new in 1975 was a service from Aberdeen to Corby, operated by Northern, jointly with Barton Transport. Northern's vehicle ran south overnight on Fridays and returned during the day on Sundays, Barton's heading north on Fridays and south on Sundays. The drivers changed over at Washington services, so that although the coaches were away from their bases on the Saturday the drivers returned home. The end-to-end trip, via Edinburgh, Barnsley, Sheffield, Nottingham, Loughborough and Leicester, was timed at 14 hours 5 minutes.

SBG frequently expressed its displeasure with the problems it encountered running rear-engined double-deckers, the Fleetlines and VRTs being less reliable than earlier generations of front-engined Titans and Lodekkas. This was a recurrent theme in the Group's annual reports in the early 1970s, and a comment from the 1972 report is typical: 'Experience with rear-engined buses remains unsatisfactory due to costly mechanical failure and too high a degree of unreliability.' This dissatisfaction was one of the factors behind the development of the Ailsa, by the Scottish-based importer of Volvo trucks. The Ailsa used a perimeter frame – novel at the time – and had a front-mounted turbocharged Volvo TD70 6.7-litre engine, at a time when the favoured power unit for SBG double-

Left **A blue-and-white livery with the fleetname 'Scottish' was the new look for London services and was applied to the motorway coaches operated by Fife and Northern, as well as those of Western SMT and Eastern Scottish, the long-established London-service operators. One of Northern's M-type Leopards climbs away from Aberdeen in 1978 at the start of the 12-hour, 550-mile overnight run to London.** STEWART J. BROWN

deckers was the ponderous but fuel-efficient 10.45-litre Gardner 6LX.

Ailsa worked with Alexander in developing a body for its new chassis, and the completed vehicle was launched at the 1973 Scottish Motor Show, in Midland livery. It entered trial service with Midland at Milngavie depot in early 1974. Milngavie was the nearest Midland depot to Ailsa Trucks' service centre at Barrhead, should the prototype require attention. A plus-point of the Ailsa, alongside its simple drivetrain, was its high carrying capacity – 79 seats. A minus-point – at least as far as the Alexander's companies were concerned – was that it was a full-height design, in fleets where every other double-deck bus (except the ex-Carmichael PD3 at Midland's Cumbernauld depot) was of low-height or lowbridge layout, and some depots were unable to accommodate full-height buses.

Fife was the first to order Ailsas, taking 40 in 1975. Fife had some history of running highbridge double-deckers with its large fleet of Guy Arabs of this layout. Initially the Ailsas were allocated to Kirkcaldy, Dunfermline and Aberhill depots. None of the Alexander's companies ordered double-deckers in 1976, but, in 1977, Fife placed another order, for 50 Ailsas. Bearing in mind that Fife only operated 220 double-deckers and had in 1970/1 taken delivery of 52 Fleetlines, the order for another 50 Ailsas – which would have meant 142 new double-deckers in eight years – was a bit surprising. In the event there was a rethink, and Fife got just six Ailsas in 1977, the remaining 44 going to other SBG companies – among them Midland, which got 14. The Midland vehicles were based in Perth for use on city services, another operation where highbridge Guy Arabs had once been common.

Northern almost got new Ailsas in 1976, as part of a plan to purchase 12 with low-height Alexander bodies. But the cramped layout of a low-height vehicle being built by Alexander for Derby Borough Transport prompted a rethink, and in place of the Ailsas Northern got 20 new Fords.

Although Northern wasn't getting new double-deckers, there was some upgrading of its fleet. In 1976, it received six Albion Lowlanders from Western SMT, joining Northern's two native examples, which, by now 13 years old, were the company's most modern double-deckers. Six eight-year-old Leopard buses went from Northern to Western in exchange. Northern also received its first rear-engined double-deckers – six of Central SMT's unwanted Fleetlines. These were the company's first Gardner-engined buses. A further 14 Fleetlines would come from Midland in 1977, displaced by that company's 14 new

Below **Rear-engined double-deckers arrived in the Northern fleet in 1976 with the acquisition of half-a-dozen five-year-old ECW-bodied Daimler Fleetlines from Central SMT. This is a September 1978 view at the depot in Gairn Terrace, Aberdeen, showing the new corporate Northern Scottish fleetname.** STEWART J. BROWN

Above **The 53-seat Leopard could by the mid-1970s be found in all three Alexander's fleets. The first Fife examples were delivered in 1974, and by 1977 the company would be running 50. This is a 1974 bus leaving Glasgow's Dundas Street bus station for Dunfermline. Fife buses provided an occasional splash of colour amidst the sea of Midland blue at Dundas Street. Long-distance services such as this catered primarily for short-distance passengers; few people would choose to sit in a bus-seated Leopard for the 2 hours 50 minutes it took to get from Glasgow to Dunfermline via Kilsyth, Stirling and Alloa.**
STEWART J. BROWN

Ailsas, and included three buses which were just 12 months old. All 20 acquired Fleetlines were allocated to Aberdeen and were used primarily on local services.

In fact the number of double-deckers in the Northern fleet had dropped significantly since the company's formation in 1961, when there had been 96, shared between seven depots. By 1978, this figure had fallen to 33 – most of them, 24, at Aberdeen, eight at Dundee and one at Montrose. The 53-seat Y-type had taken over from 53-seat lowbridge Titans and had ended double-deck operation at Elgin, Peterhead, Rosehearty and Stonehaven, although in some of those depots it would later return. In 1975, however, the ageing facilities at Rosehearty were replaced by a new depot at Fraserburgh, five miles to the east. Its initial allocation was 25 vehicles.

All three Alexander's companies continued to receive Y-type Leopards, and from 1974 all were 53-seat buses. The days of the Y-type as a coach had come to an end. For coach operation there were two alternatives, which were

chosen by all three companies – the Duple Dominant and the new Alexander T-type. Leopards with Duple Dominant bodies were delivered to Midland and Northern in 1977 and to Fife in 1978. Fife took just one batch of Dominants – 30 in total, comprising a mixture of Dominant I and Dominant II models (the latter having a deeper windscreen). However, both Midland and Northern took repeat deliveries of Dominant-bodied Leopards until 1981.

The Alexander T-type in its original incarnation was more a dual-purpose vehicle than a pure coach and was well suited to long-distance services. Midland took batches of T-type Leopards from 1978 through to 1982; Northern took T-types in 1979 and 1980, Fife in 1982. The layout of the body mouldings on the T-type saw liveries being modified to suit. Between them the three Alexander's companies took 60 T-type bodies on Leopard chassis.

The Leopards being delivered in the mid-1970s were still being supplied with manual gearboxes, but change was in the air, and from 1977 all new Leopards were specified with Pneumocyclic gearboxes. A detail change on the Y-type body from 1979 was a wider entrance – 45 inches instead of 34 inches – with twin jack-knife doors, designed to improve accessibility. Seating capacity remained unchanged at 53.

A bigger change was the arrival of the integral Leyland National. This had been in production since 1972, but SBG had avoided its complexity, and in so doing had also kept the Alexander coachbuilding plant busy producing Y-types. In 1978, Nationals were delivered to Fife (13) and Midland (15). Such was the inflexibility of the National factory at Workington that the buses were supplied in all-over red or blue, Fife and Midland applying cream relief before placing them in service. The 11.3m National seated 52 – one less than an 11m Leopard – but had a wide two-step entrance (the Y-type had three steps) and a relatively low floor level. The National's interior was clinical versus the Y-type's homely.

Right **In 1972, Midland decided that it was inappropriate to apply coach livery to its 53-seat Leopard buses. Older vehicles were then repainted blue, rather than cream, and new buses were delivered in blue. Here one of the first batch of new blue 53-seaters leaves Edinburgh for Callander in the summer of 1973. The revised style of grille was introduced in 1972.**
STEWART J. BROWN

Left By the mid-1970s it had become clear that, good as the Y-type was, it was no longer ideal for front-line coach duties; the design had, after all, been around for almost 15 years. Consequently the three Alexander's companies started placing coach orders with Duple, which bodied Fords and Leopards for all three. Midland would build up a fleet of 32 Fords with Duple Dominant bodies; its last, delivered in 1978, were five short R1014 models, one of which is seen on a private hire in Oban when new.
STEWART J. BROWN

The first Nationals were powered by Leyland's 500-series engine, a unit prone to noise and to visible smoke emissions, and not universally popular with bus engineers. Leyland was developing a Mk 2 version, with the more popular 680 engine, as used in the Leopard, and it was this which would feature in future orders.

Whatever dissatisfaction there was with the Fleetline, it was only Fife that continued to buy Ailsas, placing a follow-on order for 20 of the revised Mk II version for delivery in 1979. This was identifiable by its raised driving position; less visible changes included improvements to the brakes and the rear axle. At the end of the 1970s Fife was running 66 Ailsas and 68 Fleetlines alongside declining numbers of Lodekkas and Lowlanders. Most double-deckers were in the south of Fife; in north Fife there were just four (three Lowlanders and a Fleetline) at Cupar and one (a Fleetline) at St Andrews. There were no double-deckers at Anstruther or Newburgh.

After taking delivery of its sole batch of Ailsas in 1977, Midland reverted to the Fleetline, taking 20 with ECW bodies in 1978, followed by a final batch of 20, bodied by Alexander, in 1980. The last of these entered service in October; they were the last new Fleetlines for a Scottish operator. They were delivered in a new livery with cream relief between decks, echoing a style tried experimentally on a few buses in 1963. The 1978 ECW bodies differed from the 10 delivered in 1970 in that they had BET-style curved windscreens.

Of greater import was the delivery in 1978 of eight ECW-bodied Fleetlines to Northern – its first new double-deckers since the two Lowlanders in 1963. They were followed in 1979 by a surprise purchase – the company's first Lodekkas. There were five, transferred from Midland, these being among the batch received from Eastern National in 1971 in exchange for VRTs. Employed mainly

on school services, they would be the last half-cab buses to be run by any of the Alexander's companies and, indeed, the last in regular service with a major Scottish operator, the last survivors not being withdrawn until 1983.

By the 1970s the two Glasgow bus stations used by the Alexander's companies were showing their age. Buchanan Street dated from 1934, Dundas Street from 1944, so both had been built when the buses using them were no more than 27ft 6in long and 7ft 6in wide. The demolition of buildings in Parliamentary Road in the early 1960s had released land which was used first for short-term parking and then as a departure point for Midland's busy summer day-tours programme, which for the previous 30 years had left from the company's offices in Cathedral Street. The bus station facilities were run-down, and a new terminus was needed. Built on the land cleared in the 1960s,

Below The biggest single batch of Dominant-bodied Leopards comprised 30 delivered to Fife in 1978. All of the Dominants delivered to the Alexander's companies were built to comply with the Government's New Bus Grant specification, which required that the coaches spend part of their time on regular bus services. Here a new Fife Leopard leaves Dunfermline for Edinburgh. STEWART J. BROWN

Buchanan bus station opened in 1977. It offered a covered concourse for passengers and sheltered departure bays for services operated by all of SBG's subsidiaries serving Glasgow. It was – and remains – Scotland's busiest bus station. When it opened, Midland had 118 peak-hour departures, compared with 144 from the city centre in 1961. This still meant an average of two buses a minute but represented a drop of almost 20% in the 16 years since the company's creation.

As the 1970s progressed there were improvements to the companies' timetables, such as the inclusion of independent operators' services, a few town-centre maps and plans of bus stations, showing departure platforms. The last item even covered small stations such as that at Crieff, which had just four stances served by four routes, and where it could not have been so very difficult for passengers to find the right bus.

The decade saw some stability in terms of vehicle policy. Large numbers of Leopards and smaller numbers of Fords made up the bulk of the companies' single-deck intake; new double-deckers were Fleetlines and Ailsas. While Alexander supplied the vast majority of bodies, Duple secured an increasing share of orders for new coaches – on Leopard and Ford chassis – and ECW supplied some of the bodywork for the Fleetlines. Unusual among the Duple-bodied Fords were seven 53-seat buses, received by Northern in 1977, which had Dominant E bodies. The Dominant E used the standard coach body shell but trimmed as a bus. The Dominant Es were delivered alongside conventional 53-seat Alexander Y-type Fords. Also in 1977, Midland received an odd batch of Y-type Leopards – 13 vehicles diverted from Western SMT – which had 53 bus seats and panoramic windows; hitherto all of Midland's 53-seat Y-type Leopards had had short window bays, and the panoramic-windowed Leopard buses were to remain unique in the fleet.

The 1970s was the decade of the Y-type, even if the body was no longer considered suitable for coach duties. At the end of 1979 there were just over 1,000 Y-types in the three fleets. Midland had 497, Northern had 305, and Fife was running 202. Y-types accounted for over 60% of the combined fleets and could be found on chassis by AEC, Albion, Bristol, Ford and Leyland.

The fleets had become significantly more modern during the decade. For example, the vehicles being withdrawn by Midland in 1970 were typically around 20 years old; 10 years later the vehicles coming out of service were 16 years old. There was a similar story at Fife and at Northern.

Two of the three fleets had also shrunk. Midland's fleet at the end of the 1970s stood at 700 buses, down from 967 in 1961. There had been cuts right across the fleet. One of the biggest depots, Larbert, saw its allocation almost halved, dropping from 120 to 65. Throughout the 1960s there had been three depots with more than 100

Left **The Leyland Leopard with Alexander Y-type bodywork featured strongly in all three of Alexander's fleets, in bus and coach form. This Midland coach, skirting the west shore of Loch Lomond in April 1977, had been new to Eastern Scottish and was one of 10 transferred to Midland in 1975. They were Midland's last Y-type coaches.**
STEWART J. BROWN

vehicles – Larbert, Milngavie and Stepps. When the 1970s ended, the biggest depot, Milngavie, had just over 90 vehicles. The composition of the fleet had also changed: double-deckers comprised more than one-third (37%) of the fleet in 1961 but accounted for just 30% in 1979.

In 1979, Midland withdrew the last of its Leyland Tiger Cubs, ending a 25-year association with the model. More significant was the end of operation of side-gangway lowbridge double-deckers, which had been a feature of Alexander's operations since the purchase of eight Leyland Titan TD1s in 1929. Lowbridge buses disappeared from the Fife fleet as early as 1972, a reflection of the allocation of Lodekkas rather than Titans to the Fife Area from 1956. The last in the Midland fleet were withdrawn in 1977, but the last of all came out of service at Northern in 1978. The final Midland and Northern buses were 1961 Titan PD3A/3s, the spiritual successors to the TD1. Their withdrawal brought to an end 49 years of Titan operation.

Fife's fleet, which had initially numbered 516 vehicles, had remained stable at around this total throughout the 1960s but had fallen to 440 by the end of the 1970s. However, one of its depots, Kirkcaldy, still had more than 100 vehicles – 111, including 63 double-deckers, the biggest double-deck allocation at any Alexander's depot at this time. Significant departures from the Fife fleet in the 1970s included the last of the Guy Arab LUFs, in 1972, bringing to a close 30 years of Guy operation by Alexander's.

Northern had suffered the smallest losses, its fleet down from 454 in 1961 to 430. The company had, of course, taken over four independent operators in the 1960s which had been running 68 vehicles between them, so that masked the reduction which had taken place

in rural services. But the company had also benefited from the discovery of oil in the North Sea, which had revitalised the region's economy and helped boost traffic.

Although the Scottish Bus Group had adopted a corporate identity for its London coach services in 1976, it had refrained from interfering with the branding of its bus-operating subsidiaries. However, in 1978 it introduced a corporate fleetname incorporating a stylised Saltire – Scotland's flag – and the word 'Scottish'. So Midland and Northern dropped the lower-case fleetnames they had been using and replaced them with new corporate Midland Scottish and Northern Scottish names. Similarly Fife, which was still using the original 1962 script fleetname, became Fife Scottish. The new fleetname was blue and had to be displayed on a cream background, which requirement prompted some minor livery adaptations.

Below **Unusual among Northern's Duple-bodied Fords were seven R1114s with Dominant E bodies. The E (for Express) used the coach body shell but fitted with bus seats, offering an alternative to the purpose-designed Dominant bus body. Northern's were 53-seaters, delivered in 1977. This Stonehaven-based bus is seen on layover in Aberdeen bus station in 1978, having arrived on the service from Dundee via Forfar.**
STEWART J. BROWN

Above **Dundas Street bus station** in Glasgow was a fairly basic terminal, as this 1975 view shows. From the left the three Midland buses, all operating on former Lawson services, are a new Ford R1014 with 45-seat Y-type body, a 1963 FLF Lodekka and a 1966 ex-Eastern National FLF. Both the Ford and former Eastern National Lodekka show the unusual style of destination display that was a Lawson characteristic, the size of the lettering reducing as a way of squeezing in extra information. STEWART J. BROWN

Right **Midland's last Fords** were five R1014s with 45-seat Y-type bodies. Delivered in 1978, they brought the total number of Fords to 69. This one is seen on a Perth city service in 1981. Midland Fords had short lives, typically being sold after eight years.

STEWART J. BROWN

Left **In 1977, Midland received 13 Leopard buses that had been intended for Western SMT. Whereas Midland's Y-type buses all had short windows, those diverted from Western had panoramic windows, which set them apart from other 53-seaters in the fleet. Here one loads in Kilsyth on the service to Airdrie in 1985; this route was created under the ScotMAP project and was a successor to former Carmichael services.** STEWART J. BROWN

Below **Among the last Fords to be added to the Northern fleet were five 45-seat Duple-bodied R1014 coaches transferred from Fife in 1979, by which time they were five years old. One pauses to pick up a passenger outside Braemar Post Office in the summer of 1983. It is bound for Aberdeen – a two-and-a-half-hour journey.**
STEWART J. BROWN

A New Era

THE 1980s STARTED WELL ENOUGH. New Bus Grant had helped fund the modernisation of all three Alexander's fleets, although that scheme was being phased out in the early years of the decade, bringing an end to what were in effect half-price buses.

There were changes too in the companies' operations, as a total review of the Scottish Bus Group's route networks was underway under ScotMAP – a refinement of the National Bus Company's Market Analysis Project. A combination of a continuing decline in passenger numbers and more efficient scheduling saw the three Alexander's fleets shrinking. By the early 1980s Fife was running 300 vehicles (compared with 516 in 1961), Midland 599 (down from 967), and Northern 317 (down from 454). In percentage terms Fife suffered the biggest loss – a 42% reduction in its fleet over two decades – caused in part by the closure of coal mines in the region. Over the same period Midland's fleet was reduced by 38%, Northern's by 30%.

Two of Fife's coal-belt depots, Kelty and Lochgelly, closed in 1978 and 1982 respectively. Rationalisation in the north of the county saw the depots at Anstruther and Cupar close in 1981, most of their duties being moved to St Andrews or Newburgh. In 1985, a new depot was opened at Glenrothes, with an initial allocation of 24 vehicles, and this took on some duties previously operated by Kirkcaldy, Cowdenbeath and Aberhill.

Aside from the ScotMAP exercise, a major change affected Midland's Glasgow-area services at the start of 1982. An Act of 1930 had established what was known as the monopoly boundary, which protected the services of Glasgow Corporation, and then the Passenger Transport Executive which succeeded it, by preventing other operators from carrying local passengers within the city boundary. Thus the buses of Midland (and other SBG companies) on inward journeys to the city could drop passengers off but could not pick any up. Likewise, on outbound services, passengers could be picked up but could not alight until the first stop after the boundary. This practice ceased in 1982, SBG services being able to carry local passengers within the city, charging the same fares as applied on PTE services.

The early 1980s saw the disappearance of a number of vehicle types. The last of Midland's LHs was withdrawn in 1982. It was the end of Bristol operation by Midland, although the very last Alexander's Bristols – RELLs at Fife and Lodekkas at Northern – survived until 1983. The last Vikings were withdrawn by Midland in 1982 and by Fife and Northern in 1983, severing a link with the Glasgow-based chassis manufacturer that could be traced back to Walter Alexander's purchase of four Albion buses – also called Vikings – in 1925. Since that time there had always been Albions in Alexander's service. Just over 50 years of Bedford operation also ended in 1982, the last being a 10-year-old ex-Aberfeldy Motor Coaches YRQ.

Another make to disappear was AEC. This was generally associated with Northern, and the last of that company's Reliances was withdrawn in 1980, although

64

Left **With Midland having shown interest in the new Metrobus, MCW decided to cultivate its potential new customer by painting a prototype in Midland livery for a transport event in Glasgow organised by Strathclyde Regional Council in 1978. The bus looked well with its polished body mouldings, even if the thistles on the destination glass might be considered a case of overkill. This bus never operated for Midland – indeed, it never operated in the UK, being shipped to Hong Kong as a demonstrator for China Motor Bus. The lettering on the side reads: 'Move into the 80s with Metrobus'. In the background (left) is one of Northern's Dominant E-type Fords.**
STEWART J. BROWN

the operation of AECs by an Alexander's company continued into 1981, when the last of Fife's examples, now 15 years old, were withdrawn.

In Dundee, Northern and Tayside Regional Transport introduced a co-ordinated Tayway service in 1980. This needed additional double-deckers, a requirement met by the acquisition of seven elderly Fleetlines – dating from 1965/6 – from Western. Northern's Dundee fleet was also temporarily boosted in 1981 by the hiring of a small number of Tayside Fleetlines, which retained Tayside's blue-and-white livery but displayed Northern fleet numbers. Indeed, one general effect of the ScotMAP exercise would be an increased requirement for double-deckers.

And there were significant changes coming in bus chassis design, which would affect two of the models favoured by the Alexander's companies – the Fleetline and the Leopard. Although both models had been updated at various times in their production lives, the basic designs dated back to the late 1950s. The original Leopard had been launched in 1959, the Fleetline in 1960.

Leyland's plan had been to replace its three double-deck models – Fleetline, Atlantean and VRT – with one integral, the Titan. Fife got as far as ordering three Titans for delivery in 1979, but these were never built. Leyland quickly got the message that most bus operators did not want an integral, and alongside the Titan it developed a new chassis, the Olympian, which was offered with a choice of Gardner or Leyland engines, and had a new gearbox, the Hydracyclic, with an integral retarder. The Olympian had a perimeter frame, like the Ailsa, and air suspension. It was designed to accept low-height bodywork – and, of course, it could be bodied by Alexander.

The impending demise of the Fleetline encouraged other manufacturers to explore chassis production, and it was to

MCW rather than Leyland that Midland turned for a successor to the Fleetline. It placed an order for three of MCW's new Metrobus chassis. These entered service in 1979 and had an unusual style of four-bay 13ft 10in-high 73-seat Alexander body which was something of a stopgap between the five-bay 1960s-style AD fitted to the company's Fleetlines and the new four-bay R-type which would be fitted to all subsequent Metrobuses. The first Metrobuses to be bodied by a builder other than MCW, they had Gardner 6LXB engines – the same as in the Fleetline – and Voith automatic transmission. The first of the three was the first Metrobus in Scotland. They were allocated to Milngavie depot.

Leyland launched its Olympian at the 1980 Motor Show, and one of the launch vehicles, with a new style of ECW

Below **Three Metrobuses were delivered to Midland in 1979 with this unique style of Alexander body. The first is seen when new in Milngavie depot in July. The Metrobus badge was an unusual feature – most Metrobuses had MCW badges. All three of the original Metrobuses were still at Milngavie in 1985 and consequently formed part of the new Kelvin fleet.**
STEWART J. BROWN

Right **In 1980 and 1981, Midland held comparative trials of different types of double-decker. Based at Milngavie, these were used on route 105, which operated between Glasgow and Drumchapel. One of the 1980 vehicles was a Mk III Ailsa borrowed from Fife and repainted in Midland blue, the TB number alongside the destination identifying it as a Trial Bus. Here it presents a sorry spectacle, its wheels, supposedly cream, quite clearly not, and a malfunction in the depot's bus wash having deposited a line of grime along the cream relief band.** STEWART J. BROWN

Below **A rather smarter trial vehicle was this ECW-bodied Leyland Olympian, seen in Glasgow in February 1981 after being exhibited on Leyland's stand for the model's launch at the 1980 Motor Show. It was numbered MRO1, recalling earlier generations of non-standard double-deckers allocated RO-series fleet numbers. In June 1981 it would be transferred to Northern, where it would retain this livery layout, Northern simply over-painting the blue with yellow. This was only the fourth Olympian built, having chassis number B45-04; B45 was Leyland's development code for the model.** STEWART J. BROWN

body, was finished in Midland livery – or, at least, Leyland's interpretation of it, which featured much less blue and much more cream. Blue was used for the lower panels and the upper-deck window surrounds and roof; the rest of the body was cream. Like the Metrobuses, this had a 6LXB engine. It entered service with Midland at Milngavie at the start of 1981 – Scotland's first Olympian – but in the summer was transferred to Northern, which had 11 Olympians with Alexander bodies on order for delivery later in the year.

Whatever the merits of the Olympian, Midland stayed with MCW, taking 10 Metrobuses in 1981 to replace the company's oldest Fleetlines. They had Alexander R-type bodies seating 78 (three more than a Fleetline) and introduced a new livery with cream lower-deck window surrounds. This livery would later be applied to a small number of Fleetlines and Ailsas.

The Leopard was still going strong, although not for much longer. Those delivered to Fife in 1980 included five with three-plus-two seating at the rear, increasing seating

capacity from 53 to 62. They were intended for use on school services. Fife would continue buying Leopards until 1982, the final deliveries being a mixture of Y-type buses and T-type coaches.

At Midland too, Leopards were still being delivered, and the company was in the unusual position of buying new Y-type Leopards to replace old ones. Like Fife, Midland was taking Y-types and T-types, but it was also buying small numbers of Duple Dominant coaches. Midland's MPE series of fleet numbers had reached 425 when the last of its new Leopards was delivered. Northern, like Midland, had new Leopards with three styles of body. In total, the three Alexander's companies bought just under 700 new PSU3 Leopards over a period of 18 years.

Midland had modified the livery applied to Y-type Leopard coaches in 1978, adding a blue skirt, echoing the scheme used on the new T-types then joining the fleet. This would be changed again in 1985 when the livery for both Y-type and T-type coaches became blue with a broad area of cream between the skirt and the waistrail. The Y-type bus livery – blue with a cream waist and side-window surrounds – continued unchanged.

Northern had become Scotland's biggest Ford user, the type constituting almost 50% of the fleet at the start of the decade, but took its last examples – five Y-type buses – in 1980. These took the type's fleet numbers to NT204, although there were never that many in operation at any one time. The Fords had performed reasonably well, but the turbocharged 5.96-litre engine had a much shorter life than a 680 in a Leopard, and, overall, the Ford used lighter, less durable components. So, as they reached 10 years in operation, Northern started withdrawing them – and in many cases replaced them with ex-Western SMT Leopards which were actually older – but more durable – than the Fords they were ousting. In 1983, no fewer than 26 M-registered Leopards were transferred from Western to Northern, replacing N-registered Fords.

As the decision was made not to continue buying Fords, Northern was looking for an alternative and evaluated two possibilities. First, in 1982, came a Dennis Lancet with a mid-mounted Perkins V8 engine, an Allison automatic gearbox and a Y-type body with an obviously high floor level. This was followed early in 1983 by a Volvo B57 – a front-engined chassis similar in concept to the R-series Ford but with a lower frame and powered by the TD70 engine, as used in the Ailsa. This too had a Y-type body – the last to be built – and was intended to be a 53-seater, but was down-seated to 51 after failing its tilt test. In comparative trials the Volvo returned fuel consumption of 10.0mpg compared with 11.2mpg for the Lancet. The B57 remained unique, but Northern would later buy a few more Lancets.

The National reappeared briefly among deliveries in 1980. The revised National 2 was 300mm longer than the original model to accommodate a front-mounted radiator, necessary to leave room at the rear for the 680 engine, which had replaced the more compact 510 unit. There were 62 buses shared between Fife (22), Midland (22) and Northern (18). But while the 680 engine was a reliable unit in the Leopard, its installation in the National 2 proved troublesome. After taking National 2s in 1980, all three Alexander's companies reverted to 53-seat Y-type Leopards for their next deliveries of new single-deck buses. Despite problems with the 680 there was no concerted campaign to change the engines, although in 1984, Fife re-engined two National 2s, one with a Gardner 6HLXB, the other with a Volvo THD100. Northern fitted a Leyland TL11H engine to one of its National 2s in 1985.

Coach operation was deregulated in 1980, opening up the operation of express services and excursions to all operators. There wasn't a lot of competition on internal

Above **For operators wanting an Alexander-bodied coach the Y-type had been supplanted by the T-type, and this model, on Leyland Leopard chassis, would be supplied to Midland from 1978, to Northern from 1979 and to Fife from 1980. A Fife Leopard is pictured in summer traffic in Perth in 1987. All three companies used T-types primarily on express or inter-urban services; Duple's Dominant had replaced the Y-type on front-line coaching duties.** STEWART J. BROWN

Left **From 1981, the standard Midland double-decker was the MCW Metrobus with 78-seat Alexander R-type bodywork. Most had Gardner 6LXB engines – as had been fitted to the Fleetlines that preceded them – although there were smaller numbers with engines by Rolls-Royce or Cummins. Here a 1985 bus approaches Kirkintilloch Cross. The livery with cream window surrounds was introduced with the first of the R-types in 1981 and echoed the layout used by Northern. When Kelvin Scottish was formed in the summer of 1985 this bus would be one of 73 Metrobuses inherited by the new company.** STEWART J. BROWN

Scottish coach services, although one newcomer, Stagecoach, introduced a number of long-distance routes, including one linking Glasgow, Perth, Dundee and Aberdeen.

Against this background coach operators were looking for a chassis which was more powerful and more sophisticated than the Leopard. Leyland's response was the Tiger, launched in 1981. The Tiger had air suspension and the more powerful 218bhp TL11H engine – a development of the previous 680, but turbocharged. Northern was the first Alexander's company to get Tigers, seven being delivered in 1982. All had Duple bodywork with small trapezoidal windows, emulating the style of the Alexander M-type; having last built an M-type in 1976, Alexander was unwilling to dust off the drawings and re-engineer the body for the small number of Tigers SBG would be specifying as London-style coaches. The seven for Northern were all finished in corporate Scottish livery, six being high-floor Goldliner III 46-seaters for London

operation, the seventh a standard-height Dominant III fitted out as a luxurious 29-seater and used to transport Aberdeen Football Club. They were followed in 1983 by five coaches with standard Dominant II 47-seat bodies. Fife's first Tigers, in 1983, were three London-specification Duple Goldliners, similar to those already in operation with Northern.

Midland received 20 Tiger coaches in 1983, with four different body styles. The first five had Alexander T-type bodies and were virtually indistinguishable from the previous year's T-type Leopards. Then came five with Dominant II bodies, followed by five with Alexander's facelifted TE – E for Express – body. This had a new windscreen, revised front panels, and an attractive new livery. The last five had TC bodies – C for Coach – which featured bonded glazing and a single-piece door. The 1983 facelift of the T transformed what had been a workmanlike express body into an altogether more modern-looking vehicle. Midland's first 15 Tigers used an optional low-powered version of the TL11H engine, rated at just 170bhp.

With each of SBG's subsidiaries operating long-distance services in Scotland under their own names, there was little public awareness of a network of routes. SBG's response to competition from Stagecoach and other newcomers was to package its subsidiaries' long-distance services under the Scottish Citylink brand, identified by a new livery of two-tone blue and yellow. This was applied to Midland's 1983 TC-bodied Tigers and to 10 Duple-bodied Tigers which followed in 1984. Some existing coaches in all three Alexander's fleets were repainted in Citylink colours, among the oldest being 1975 M-type Leopards in the Fife and Northern fleets.

Before Citylink was launched, one T-type Leopard coach in each of the Fife and Midland fleets was repainted in a cream-and-silver livery with prominent Cityliner

branding. This was not pursued, although the Cityliner name was taken up by Western for some of its express services. A silver-based livery would later, in 1987, be used by Fife for Volvo Citybuses on the Edinburgh-Leven service, branded as Fife Coastliner.

What became the Citylink livery had first been seen at the 1982 Motor Show, on an MCW Metroliner double-deck coach which although owned by MCW was delivered to Northern for use on the Aberdeen-London service. The three-axle 12m-long Metroliner was an impressive-looking vehicle and seated 69 passengers – 50% more than the 46 on a 12m London-specification Leyland Tiger. It was powered by a 290bhp Cummins L10 engine, driving through a Voith gearbox. Two more similar coaches would follow. But, however good it looked, the Metroliner was not the most reliable of vehicles. And if one broke down on the M6 or M1 motorways in England on its way to or from London, two replacement coaches would be needed to rescue its passengers. Northern's three double-deck Metroliners would be transferred to Western in 1989.

At the same time as it unveiled the Metroliner double-decker MCW announced a 12m rear-engined single-deck coach, also called Metroliner. The body was square, MCW's trademark asymmetrical windscreen adding the merest touch of style. Northern took two in 1984 (of a production run of just 11 coaches). They had Cummins L10 engines, like the double-decker, but with a lower 250bhp power rating, and SCG Hydracyclic gearboxes, which were later replaced by Voith units to improve reliability. A significantly restyled Hi-liner version of the Metroliner single-deck coach had been introduced in 1984, and Northern took seven in 1985/6. These had Voith transmission from the outset. The last two single-deck Metroliners were in Northern livery; the first seven were Citylink coaches.

In the late 1970s and at the start of the 1980s there had been a fairly straightforward approach to buying coaches, 90 Duple Dominant-bodied Leopards being delivered to the three companies. However, with the arrival of the Tiger, the end of the Dominant and the launch of Citylink a much more fragmented approach was adopted, in part as the companies started taking coaches to different specifications for different types of work – as demonstrated by Midland's 20 Tigers in 1983. By 1987, when the last of 83 Tiger coaches were delivered, Fife would have 13, Midland 45 and Northern 25, 40 of them being in Citylink colours.

Among the more unusual Leyland coach deliveries were four Royal Tiger Doyen rear-engined integrals – two each for Fife and Northern. The Fife coaches were diverted from Western. The Doyen was built at the Roe factory in Leeds, and these coaches were 46-seaters, delivered in 1984 in corporate Scottish livery for London service operation, although all four were soon repainted in Citylink colours.

Above **All three Alexander's companies added National 2s to their fleets. Midland had 21, all 11.6m 52-seaters delivered in 1980. This one is seen in Glasgow in 1985. The route number in the 170s serves as a reminder that this was once a Lawson service, even if the Lawson company had been gone for 24 years.**

STEWART J. BROWN

Although the Tiger was conceived primarily as a coach chassis, a bus version was also available, and this was chosen by Fife and Northern, which between them took 27, with Alexander P-type bodies. The 14 for Northern included seven with Gardner 6HLXB engines, which was not such a strange choice as it first appeared, as Northern had standardised on Gardner-powered Olympians for its double-deck fleet. And among Fife's 13 Tiger buses were eight 12m-long 61-seaters, at a time when the use of maximum-length vehicles on bus services was unusual. They were the only 12m service buses for an Alexander's company. After two decades of the stylish Y-type, with its curved windscreens, the P-type was angular, with flat-glass screens. The body had been designed with an eye on export markets, which compromised its appearance for UK buyers – not that there were many. Along with the Tigers, Northern took its last lightweight buses – five Perkins-engined Dennis Lancets, also with P-type bodies. Midland bought no new full-size single-deck buses after its last Leopards in 1982.

Variety in coaches was not quite matched by variety in double-deckers. The picture at Midland was straightforward: MCW Metrobuses. Deliveries of Metrobuses with R-type bodies had started in 1981 and continued every year until 1987, by which time Midland had bought 121, including the three early, pre-R-type buses. Most had Gardner engines, but there were seven with Rolls-Royce engines (shared between Milngavie and Grangemouth depots) and 22 powered by the Cummins L10, which were allocated to half a dozen depots.

Northern too had a standardised approach, favouring the Leyland Olympian. After taking 10 with Alexander bodies in 1981 it switched to ECW bodywork for 21 delivered in 1982. These would be the last ECW bodies for the company; all subsequent Olympians would have Alexander bodywork. Early Olympian chassis were built in Bristol, so although SBG had abandoned Bristol as a supplier of double-deck buses after the VRT debacle, Northern's first 43 Olympians (including the ex-Midland prototype) were Bristol-built. Its later Olympians were produced at the Leyland National factory in Workington. One odd Olympian was delivered in 1985, fitted with a five-cylinder Gardner 5LXCT in place of the standard 6LXB. It remained unique; Gardner's long period of popularity as a supplier of engines to the bus industry was coming to an end. From 1984, meanwhile, Northern had specified Voith transmission in place of the Leyland Hydracyclic used on the earlier vehicles.

In the 18 years from 1961 to 1978, Northern had received just 17 new double-deck buses; in the seven years from 1981 to 1987 it took 88. This was in part a reflection of a growing presence on city services in Aberdeen. In 1983, Northern and Grampian Regional Transport launched a co-ordinated service network in the Aberdeen area. The vehicles used by Northern – mainly Olympians – were painted in Grampian's green-and-cream livery with Grampian Scottish fleetnames. This livery was applied to all 15 new Olympians delivered in 1983/4 and to six of those supplied in 1985. For the Grampian Scottish operation Northern also acquired four Leyland-engined Fleetlines from Grampian Transport, in 1983. These were 10-year-old dual-door buses and, of course, did not have to be repainted. They were transferred in 1985 to Strathtay, where they would find use in Perth, initially still in Grampian colours. The big intake of double-deckers in the 1980s saw Olympians allocated to most Northern depots, including some that had not previously seen double-deckers – among them Blairgowrie and Macduff, each of which had two.

Fife had the most varied approach to double-deckers. In 1983, it tried a Leyland Olympian demonstrator and then took 10 Olympians with Gardner engines and R-type bodies. These were its first new double-deckers since 1979 and its only new Leyland double-deckers. These were followed in 1984 by eight Ailsas; these had Mk III chassis and Alexander R-type bodies. The Olympians seated 77, the Ailsas 81. The Olympians, divided between Kirkcaldy and Cowdenbeath, revived the FRO classification last seen on Guy Arabs in 1970.

The Ailsa was at this time being phased out by Volvo in favour of the mid-engined Citybus, developed from its popular B10M coach chassis. The Citybus had a horizontal 9.6-litre Volvo THD100 engine and a Voith gearbox. The first for Fife were two 11.7m-long double-deck coaches, with Alexander RVC bodywork – unique to Fife but similar to the two RLC bodies built at around the same time on Olympian chassis for Eastern Scottish. Based on the standard R-type frame, the 70-seat RVC had bonded tinted glazing and a coach-style front end. The pair entered service in 1984 in Citylink livery, initially on the Perth-Edinburgh route, but in 1985 were repainted in fleet colours for use on express services to Glasgow; in 1987 they were transferred to Western Scottish.

These two strange coaches were followed by conventional Citybuses, starting with 10 in 1984. A further 21 followed in 1986, and a final pair, diverted from Western in exchange for the RVC coaches, arrived in 1987. These all had Alexander R-type bodies, as had a former Volvo demonstrator which joined the fleet in 1986.

Second-hand vehicles were unusual in the Alexander's fleets. In 1983, Fife needed additional vehicles for school contracts and purchased six second-hand Fleetlines, three each from Grampian and Tayside. These were full-height, dual-door buses, new in 1973. The Tayside buses were long-wheelbase models, while those from Grampian had Leyland engines. All were based at Newburgh and operated until 1987. Even more unusual acquisitions in the following year were the company's first Atlanteans – 10 Alexander-bodied AN68s from Grampian. These 11-year-old buses, also with dual-door Alexander bodies, were used on services in the south of Fife and started a new FRN class. All of the dual-door buses later had their centre exits removed and were up-seated, the 33ft ex-Tayside Fleetlines becoming 86-seaters – the highest-capacity buses operated by any Alexander's company.

Above **A Northern National 2 stands in Fraserburgh bus station, ready to depart for nearby Rosehearty on a service once operated by Simpson's with second-hand double-deckers. Northern had 18 National 2s, of which 12, including this vehicle, were 11.6m 52-seaters. The Nationals were new in 1980; this is a 1987 view, with 'Best Bus' branding featuring prominently.** STEWART J. BROWN

Left **Fife also received 21 National 2s in 1980, these comprising long and short versions. This is a short (10.6m) 44-seater, one of 10, all of which were based in Dunfermline. It is seen leaving the town's bus station in 1987. Fife had by now adopted a large-sized fleetname and was using a version of the Scottish Bus Group's 'Best Bus' deregulation marketing campaign – 'Best Bus in the Kingdom'. The company was at this time facing competition from Rennie's of Dunfermline, owner of the Scania/MCW Metropolitan parked behind the National. Both Fife and Rennie's would ultimately become part of the Stagecoach group.** STEWART J. BROWN

Above **In 1983, Midland took 20 Leyland Tigers, with four different styles of body. The first five entered service in January and had Alexander T-type bodies which were little different from those fitted to earlier Leopard chassis. One is seen in Aviemore when new, on the service from Glasgow to Inverness.** STEWART J. BROWN

Right **Just three months later, in April, Midland took delivery of a further five Tigers, this time with Alexander's updated TE body, the 'E' indicating Express. The front and rear were restyled, the side mouldings revised, and the livery changed to suit. It was a remarkable transformation, as demonstrated by this coach as it prepares to depart Glasgow for Inverness and Nairn in June 1983.**
STEWART J. BROWN

Left **Good as the TE upgrade was, for real coach style Duple had the edge. Five of the 1983 Midland Tigers had impressive Dominant II coach bodies. These had simpler side mouldings than earlier Dominants for Midland, as well as a revised livery. This one is seen in Blackpool in 1984, 12 months old but still sparkling like new.** STEWART J. BROWN

Below **A further upgrade of the Alexander T-type was available in the form of the TC (C for Coach), which featured tinted square-cornered glazing and the option of a single-piece plug door. Fife took five on Leyland Tiger chassis in 1985. This one is seen in 1987 on a private hire in Manchester, with the approved SBG corporate name on the front but a non-standard version on the side.** STEWART J. BROWN

Right **Among the more unusual coaches to wear Citylink livery was this former London-service Leopard, with Alexander M-type body, in the Northern fleet. It has been fitted with power-operated jack-knife doors and is seen in Inverness bus station in September 1983, shortly before the 1 October launch of the Citylink brand – the lettering on the side reads simply 'Scottish', followed by a space to which 'Citylink' will be added. It offered a high standard of comfort on the service to Aberdeen.** STEWART J. BROWN

Below **Cityliner branding was tried in 1983 by both Fife and Midland, on a couple of T-type coaches, the cream-and-silver livery being relieved by stripes of red or blue as appropriate. Midland's example – a 12-month-old Leopard – is pictured near Ratho station on the Edinburgh-Stirling service.** STEWART J. BROWN

Left **What would become Citylink livery was first seen in 1982 on an MCW Metroliner demonstrator that was operated by Northern on the Aberdeen-London service. The 69-seat coach was purchased by Northern in 1984 and would later be joined by two similar vehicles. The Metroliner was not the most successful of designs, and all three were transferred to Western in 1989.** STEWART J. BROWN

Below **MCW's brief foray into the single-deck coach market in the 1980s produced two quite different rear-engined models marketed under the Metroliner name. The first was the least successful, and Northern had two. They were 48-seaters with toilets and were in Citylink livery. The longest Citylink service linked Aberdeen and Plymouth, the location of this 1984 photograph, a distance of some 630 miles.** MARK BAILEY

Right **Two Leyland Royal Tiger Doyen integral coaches, intended for Western SMT, were instead delivered to Fife in 1984. They were originally in blue-and-white London-service livery but were later repainted in Citylink colours, as seen in London's Victoria Coach Station in 1987, where the absence of a boarding platform appears to be presenting quite a challenge to an elderly traveller.**
STEWART J. BROWN

Below **Northern also got two Doyens, which like those at Fife were 46-seaters with toilets and were built by Roe. They were delivered in corporate Scottish livery. This one is seen when new in Plymouth – about as far from Aberdeen as it could get on the British mainland.**
MARK BAILEY

Above **The standard Northern double-decker in the 1980s was the Gardner-engined Leyland Olympian. The first 10, delivered in 1981, had Alexander R-type bodies. Here one crosses the granite setts of Guild Street Bridge in Aberdeen, operating on a local service to Torry.**
STEWART J. BROWN

Left **The 21 Olympians delivered to Northern in 1982 had 77-seat ECW bodies, the last for the company. This view shows clearly the blue lining which had been added to the livery applied to Nationals and Olympians.**
GAVIN BOOTH

Above **In 1983, Northern and Grampian Regional Transport introduced a co-ordinated service network in Aberdeen, using the Grampian Scottish name. This saw Northern operating a number of vehicles – mainly Olympians – in Grampian livery and equipping them with fareboxes. The co-ordination would be short-lived, for the deregulation of local bus services in 1986 turned the partners into competitors. This Alexander-bodied bus was one of 21 Olympians delivered in Grampian Scottish livery between 1983 and 1985.** STEWART J. BROWN

Above right **For school contracts Fife purchased six Daimler Fleetlines from Tayside and Grampian in 1983. All were dual-door buses with full-height Alexander bodies. An ex-Grampian bus is seen soon after acquisition in Cupar, on a lunchtime trip to Newburgh. These vehices would later have their centre exits removed.** STEWART J. BROWN

Below right **Unusual second-hand purchases by Fife in 1984 were 10 Leyland Atlanteans from Grampian Regional Transport. This is a 1987 view in Perth, showing the brighter livery adopted from 1986. Previously these buses had been all-over red with a single band of cream above the lower-deck windows. When they joined the Fife fleet they had two doors, but they were soon rebuilt as shown and up-seated from 74 to 81. They briefly carried FRF fleet numbers in the series for Daimler Fleetlines before being numbered in a new FRN series.** GAVIN BOOTH

Changing Times

6

THE MID-1980S SAW MASSIVE CHANGES in the bus industry nationwide, as the established system of bus-route licensing was abolished in 1986, opening up the market to competition. In anticipation of this the Scottish Bus Group restructured its operating subsidiaries in 1985, and this affected two of the three Alexander's companies. All of the company names were changed. W. Alexander & Sons (Midland) Ltd became Midland Scottish Omnibuses Ltd, the Fife and Northern companies being re-titled in similar fashion.

Fife's operating area remained unchanged, but not so those of Midland and Northern. First there was a reallocation in March 1985 of Eastern Scottish's Glasgow-area services, operated from its depot at Baillieston. That depot was closed, and the 43 buses and coaches based there were transferred to Midland's Stepps depot, in advance of the main Group restructuring which would follow in June. All of the vehicles retained their Eastern Scottish fleet numbers and livery but received Midland Scottish fleetnames and legal lettering.

The June changes were extensive, representing the biggest upheaval in SBG's history. Midland's southern area, including its depots at Milngavie, Kirkintilloch, Kilsyth, Stepps and Cumbernauld, were transferred to a new Kelvin Scottish company, which also acquired the Central Scottish operations at Old Kilpatrick, which were separate from the rest of the Central business. In addition, Midland lost its operations in Perthshire, the depots at

Crieff, Perth and Pitlochry going to a new Strathtay Scottish company.

There were some gains at Midland. Among these it regained its Oban depot, which had been transferred to Highland in 1970. This brought with it 20 single-deck buses – an increase over the 14 that had been based there 15 years earlier, thanks to the addition of former MacBrayne operations, which now saw Midland buses running as far north as Fort William. The buses at Oban were mainly Leopards and Fords. Midland also took over operations on Islay, where Western had been operating since 1979; this brought five mid-1970s Leyland Leopards which had been new to Paton of Renfrew, a company acquired by Western in 1979. Finally the Eastern Scottish depot at Linlithgow, along with 26 Seddon Pennines, came under Midland control. Most of the Seddons had Alexander bodywork, but there were two bodied by Plaxton, a manufacturer whose products had never featured strongly in the Midland fleet. The Gardner-engined Seddon was a new chassis type for Midland.

The net result of the June changes was that Midland, which just under 25 years earlier had been running 967 vehicles from 16 depots in an area extending from Glasgow to Perth, was reduced to 292 vehicles running in central Scotland from eight depots, at Alloa, Balfron, Bannockburn, Grangemouth, Islay, Larbert, Linlithgow and Oban.

The Linlithgow Seddons were not quite the first examples of that make in the Midland fleet, as earlier in the

Above **A minor reorganisation in March 1985 saw the Eastern Scottish operations at Baillieston being transferred to Midland at Stepps. It was a short-term measure, ahead of the major changes taking place in June, so none of the vehicles was repainted. However, all received Midland Scottish fleetnames, creating for a few months the sight of green-liveried Midland buses in Glasgow. This is an ECW-bodied Leyland Olympian, which, like the rest of the former Baillieston fleet, would pass to the new Kelvin Scottish company.** STEWART J. BROWN

Left **The June 1985 reorganisation saw Midland taking over the Eastern Scottish Linlithgow depot and with it a fleet of 26 Seddon Pennines. Most had Alexander Y-type bodies, and were being repainted as a new version of Midland's livery, with blue skirt, roof and window surrounds, was being introduced for dual-purpose Y-types. This one is seen leaving Edinburgh for Linlithgow.**
STEWART J. BROWN

year the company had acquired a solitary Pennine VII from Western. This had been adapted to carry a wheelchair, with a lift fitted in mid-wheelbase. As rebuilt it was a 24-seater and was based at Alloa. The Seddons created a new MSE class. Midland had also (briefly) ran 11 that were acquired with Eastern's Baillieston operations, although these were not allocated fleet numbers.

Before 1985 was out, Midland took over from Clydeside its Ardrishaig-based operations – three Tigers on Scottish Citylink services, plus three Seddons. These were former MacBrayne services, which had been acquired by Western SMT when MacBrayne's operations were being absorbed by SBG at the start of the 1970s. Midland pulled out of Ardrishaig in 1987, the operation being taken over by West Coast Motors of Campbeltown; in exchange Midland took on West Coast's Oban-Easdale service and a Benderloch school contract. The five-vehicle Islay operation ended in 1986 when the contracts to run the island's bus services were lost to Mundell, a local haulier which diversified into buses.

The changes at Northern were simpler. It was basically reshaped to serve Grampian Region, its southern depots at Blairgowrie, Dundee, Forfar, Arbroath and Montrose joining Midland's former Perthshire operations in the new Strathtay company. This left Northern with 254 buses (down from 454 in 1961) and depots at Aberdeen, Buckie, Elgin, Fraserburgh, Macduff, Peterhead and Stonehaven.

Strathtay commenced operations with 127 vehicles – 64 from Midland and 63 from Northern. It established its headquarters in Dundee and adopted a striking new orange-and-blue livery, soon modified by the addition of white relief. Kelvin started out with a livery of two-tone blue, but this was quickly changed, the company experimenting with various styles before settling on a

much brighter two-tone blue and yellow. The use of Midland blue by both Kelvin and Strathtay reflected an SBG edict that the new companies created in 1985 should use liveries which in some way acknowledged their heritage.

The slimmed-down Midland continued buying Metrobuses, albeit fewer of them, along with a handful of small buses. These latter comprised four MCW Metroriders – the first in Scotland – for operation in Alloa and two Freight Rover Sherpas, with unusual Portuguese-built Elme Orion bodies, for a Strathclyde PTE contract in the Oban area. This served Bonawe, using a road with a 14-seat limit for buses. The Sherpas were able to run as 14-seaters on the PTE contract but could be operated with 16 seats when used on other duties. Midland ordered

Below **Midland briefly operated on Islay in 1985/6, using five Leyland Leopards which Western had been running on the island since 1979. They had been new to Paton of Renfrew, and this one is seen in Oban after Midland lost its Islay contracts. It has a Duple Dominant E bus body.**
STEWART J. BROWN COLLECTION

Above **A Y-type in Midland's dual-purpose livery has the Strathtay name on the side but still claims to be a Midland bus on the front. It is one of the vehicles which had been diverted from Western SMT and thus started life as a panoramic-windowed 53-seat bus – a rare type in the Midland fleet – but was later fitted with 49 dual-purpose seats, thereby becoming a standard type. It is seen pausing outside Blackford parish church on its way from Stirling to Perth in August 1985.** STEWART J. BROWN

Right **Two of the Linlithgow Seddons had Plaxton bodies – rare in the Midland fleet – and these were joined in 1987 by two more, transferred from Kelvin. This ex-Kelvin coach had been new to Eastern in 1979 and originally had a T-suffix registration; it was among a large number of Midland coaches re-registered with 'dateless' numbers in the late 1980s.**
STEWART J. BROWN

four Renault minibuses, with Alexander bodies, in 1987, but these were cancelled before delivery. Instead it gained four Mercedes-Benz L608D van conversions, transferred from Kelvin; these were 12 months old and were for use on Alloa and Linlithgow town services.

In 1988, Midland closed its Grangemouth depot, the work being transferred to Larbert. In the same year it vacated the former Alexander's head office in Brown Street, Camelon, transferring its administration to offices at Larbert depot. Two former Alexander's workshop buildings remain in Brown Street, but the greater part of the site is now occupied by a residential care home.

A significant change for Northern was the ending of the Grampian Scottish agreement; deregulation was approaching, and the Government's stated aim was to foster competition between bus operators. Northern rose to the challenge by specifying dual-door bodywork on 18 Olympians delivered in 1987, the better to compete with Grampian Regional Transport, which had standardised on dual-door buses since the days of predecessor Aberdeen Corporation Transport in the mid-1960s. The dual-door Olympians displayed City Bus branding on a new livery of cream, yellow and blue. Northern's expansion in Aberdeen was matched by GRT's

Left **Strathtay initially adopted a distinctive orange-and-blue livery, seen on an ex-Midland Leopard unloading in Perth in 1986. Strathtay inherited 22 Leopards from Midland. Although originally a 53-seat bus, this vehicle has been re-equipped with 49 coach seats.** STEWART J. BROWN

Below **The Strathtay livery was soon modified by the addition of white relief. This Leyland Tiger with Alexander's boxy P-type body was one of four acquired from Northern in 1987 in exchange for Leyland Nationals. It is seen in Perth soon after joining the Strathtay fleet.** STEWART J. BROWN

Above **The new Kelvin company's initial fleet included 73 ex-Midland Metrobuses. This bus passing through Riddrie, in the east of Glasgow, wears the first version of Kelvin's livery, albeit with the addition of a yellow front.** STEWART J. BROWN

Right **Kelvin later adopted various blue and yellow schemes, one version of which is seen on an ex-Midland Leyland Tiger heading through Cumbernauld on its way from Dunfermline to Glasgow in 1987. This coach is from the same batch as the vehicle illustrated in Midland service on page 73. It is just four years old, and its demotion from front-line touring to inter-urban service has been rapid.** STEWART J. BROWN

introduction of competition on some out-of-town services, and its last new double-deckers in SBG ownership were five coach-seated Olympians delivered in 1987. Having had no Gardner-engined buses in 1976, Northern was now running around 100, these making up 40% of its fleet. The last additions to the Northern fleet in SBG days were 21 assorted minibuses – 12 Renaults from Central and nine Mercedes L608Ds from seven different operators.

There was also competition for Northern from a new company which cheekily traded as Alexander's – following the name changes in 1985 there were no longer any Alexander's bus companies to complain. The Alexander (North East) company started running coaches on services from Aberdeen to Peterhead and Fraserburgh in November 1988, but it was losing money from the start and called in the receivers 12 months later. In the meantime it had, in April 1989, taken over the operations of the short-lived Inverness Traction business, which had started in May 1988. Parts of the operations of both Alexander (North East) and Inverness Traction were taken over by Stagecoach in November 1989.

Fife bought significant numbers of minibuses – 20 MCW Metroriders in 1988 for Buzz Bus services in Kirkcaldy and 24 Renault S56s in the period 1987-9, largely to counter competition from Moffat & Williamson in Glenrothes and from Rennie's in Dunfermline. Most of the Renaults had Alexander bodies, but the last four were bodied by Reeve Burgess.

In 1987, Fife abandoned the alphanumeric fleet numbering system it had inherited from Alexander's, instead adopting blocks of numbers to identify different types of vehicle. The company had earlier (for a brief period

in 1980/1) dropped the F prefix from its fleet numbers but had soon reinstated it. The new system saw Leopard buses keep their original numbers, minus the FPE prefix, Leopard dual-purpose vehicles being numbered in the 2xx series (by adding 100 to their existing fleet numbers). The other principal number series were 3xx for Nationals, 4xx and 5xx for Tigers, 7xx for Fleetlines and Olympians, 8xx for Ailsas and 9xx for Citybuses.

By contrast, while Fife was abandoning Alexander's-style fleet numbers the new Strathtay company acknowledged its Alexander's heritage by using fleet numbers which included an S prefix before a second letter indicating the vehicle type, eg SF for Strathtay Ford; this echoed the introduction a quarter of a century earlier of F, M and N prefixes by the then new Fife, Midland and Northern companies.

Above **The first production MCW Metroriders entered service with Midland in the early months of 1987. There were four, each fitted with 26 coach seats, and they were based initially at Alloa, for use on local services. This one, with prominent Bluebird name, is loading for Tullibody, with an MCW Metrobus bound for Stirling behind it. Fife also bought Metroriders.** STEWART J. BROWN

Left **After deregulation in 1986, Northern started competing in Aberdeen with Grampian Regional Transport, introducing a new livery of blue, yellow and cream with City Bus branding. This 1985 Olympian is seen in Castle Street – once the hub of Aberdeen Corporation's services – in 1987. It displays a C, for City, depot code rather than A for Aberdeen.** STEWART J. BROWN

Above **Towards the end of its days as a Scottish Bus Group subsidiary Northern added blue to its livery and placed a new emphasis on the Bluebird name, which had been dropped after the 1961 split. Northern took Leyland Tigers with Alexander P-type bodies in 1983 and 1984, the later vehicles, one of which is seen here on the Fraserburgh town service, having Gardner rather than Leyland engines. These would be Northern's last new single-deck buses.**
STEWART J. BROWN

Right **The last new Leylands for an Alexander's company were five Tigers delivered to Northern in 1987; Walter Alexander had first bought Leylands in 1919, and Tigers of one sort or another had been purchased from 1929. The final Tigers had 57-seat Alexander TC bodies with tinted glazing and a plug door. Attitudes towards smoking were changing in the 1980s, and while Northern did not ban smoking it did banish smokers to the rear of the coach, as indicated by the 'No smoking' signs applied to the side windows which do not extend to the last few rows of seats.** STEWART J. BROWN

In its six years in SBG ownership Strathtay bought 33 new vehicles. That its 17 new double-deckers comprised nine Olympians and eight Metrobuses is a pointer to the company's dual parentage. For urban services in Dundee and Perth it bought 26 Routemasters from London Buses, the bulk of them in 1986. In 1989, six were repainted dark red and given Perth City Transport fleetnames, a reminder of the use of ex-London Guys in Alexander's Perth city fleet in the 1950s and early 1960s. The Routemasters were used to combat growing competition from Stagecoach, which introduced Perth Panther services to the city in 1989.

For Citylink operation Strathtay bought three new coaches – one Tiger with Alexander TC body and two Royal Tiger Doyens. Its last new buses – and, indeed, the last new buses for any SBG company – were 13 Renault S56s bought from the stock of Birmingham-based dealer Carlyle and, uniquely for new SBG vehicles, registered in England. These had 25-seat Dormobile Routemaker bodies and were for use in Perth as part of Strathtay's drive to protect itself from Stagecoach. They displayed City Nipper branding on a red livery.

As if on-street competition were not a big enough problem, SBG was faced with the prospect of privatisation. The Group lobbied, unsuccessfully, for its sale as a single unit, and in the end had to advertise each subsidiary for sale individually. It was a slow process. Privatisation was announced in January 1988, but it would be June 1990 before any sales were completed.

Above **Fife had traditionally painted Y-type buses in all-over red, with cream relief limited to the waistband and, on some vehicles, the window surrounds. That changed dramatically in 1986, when the company began repainting Y-type Leopards in a livery similar to that used on its Nationals. The result was impressive and was helped by the bold fleetname, as seen on two Leopards on local services in Dunfermline.** STEWART J. BROWN

Left **Newspapers and parcels played an important part in Alexander's business over the years. In this 1987 view in Aberdeen bus station piles of newspapers wait to be loaded onto country-service buses. The wicker basket was used to move newspapers and parcels around the bus station. The coach is a 1983 Duple-bodied Leyland Tiger.** STEWART J. BROWN

Right **Scottish Bus Group companies were not strong on marking anniversaries, which made Fife's commemoration of 50 years since the end of Dunfermline's trams all the more remarkable. A Volvo Citybus with Alexander R-type body was repainted in an approximation of the Dunfermline & District Traction Co's livery in 1987 and even had the FRA prefix dropped from its fleet number, displaying simply the number 93 in gold tramway-style lettering. The split-step entrance was an early attempt at improving access for people with impaired mobility.**
STEWART J. BROWN

Right **In 1987, Fife adopted Coastliner branding for its service between Leven and Edinburgh. This is a 1986 Volvo Citybus with Alexander body, leaving St Andrew Square bus station in Edinburgh. It is the same location as the Fife Guy Arab LUF on page 28, but in the intervening 20 years an office block has been built over the bus station exit. This bus was originally part of the FRA class, but by 1989, when this photograph was taken, Fife had adopted a new fleet-numbering system that dispensed with class codes.**
MARK BAILEY

Left **In the 1950s Alexander's had operated 25 ex-London Transport Guys on Perth city services, and many were still in use when the new Midland company was formed in 1961. Former London buses in Scottish Bus Group ownership returned to the streets of Perth in 1987, in the shape of Routemasters owned by Strathtay. A few were later repainted in red Perth City Transport livery. Strathtay had 26 Routemasters for operation in Perth and Dundee.**
STEWART J. BROWN

Left **This view inside the former Midland depot at Perth illustrates Strathtay's mixed heritage, with two Fleetlines (one of them new to Midland) in Northern livery, an ex-Midland Ailsa, two former Grampian Transport Fleetlines and two ex-Midland Fleetlines which are in the new company's colours. At the far end of the line-up is a preserved Alexander's Titan PD3.**
GAVIN BOOTH

The End of Alexander's

Above **Eight Scania N113CRLs with 49-seat Wright bodies joined the Midland Bluebird fleet in 1995, as FirstBus perpetuated predecessor GRT's policy of raising the quality of the fleet. One is seen leaving Edinburgh for Linlithgow, on a service previously operated by Seddon Pennines. It displays an Alexander's-style 'Lw' (Linlithgow) depot-allocation code below the nearside windscreen.** STEWART J. BROWN

MIDLAND, BY NOW RUNNING 280 buses and coaches and trading as Bluebird, was the first of the former Alexander's companies to be sold. It went in September 1990 to GRT Holdings, set up by the recently privatised Grampian Regional Transport, for £8.5 million, doubling the size of GRT's operations. GRT adopted the trading name Midland Bluebird and introduced a livery of bright cream and two-tone blue – a marked improvement on the scheme it replaced, which by the standards of the 1990s was looking a bit old-fashioned. In 1993, the company would be formally renamed Midland Bluebird – a name which continues to this day. An unusual feature of the Midland Bluebird fleet after it was privatised was the re-registering of vehicles – mainly coaches – with 'dateless' registration marks, and by 1992 more than 60 coaches – the bulk of the coach fleet – had been re-registered. An early sign of the change of ownership was the transfer to Midland Bluebird of 14-year-old Alexander-bodied Atlanteans to speed the withdrawal of Fleetlines. Investment in new buses in the 1990s would focus on Wright-bodied Scanias. In 1991, GRT closed the company's Alloa depot, where the allocation had shrunk from 60 vehicles in 1961 to barely 20 three decades later. The Oban operation was sold by GRT in December 1992, to a new Oban & District company, which would later (in 1999) be acquired by West Coast Motors.

Northern was bought by Stagecoach in March 1991, for £5.7 million. In the run-up to privatisation the company had begun trading as Bluebird Northern, the name Moray Bluebird being used on some Elgin-area vehicles, and Buchan Bluebird on some buses in the Peterhead and Fraserburgh areas. Stagecoach formally renamed the company as Bluebird Northern in March 1992, and then again as Bluebird Buses in October of the same year, finally severing the link with the Northern name after just over 30 years. One of the first moves by Stagecoach was to introduce a substantial fleet of modern minibuses, 23 one-year-old Mercedes 709Ds with Alexander bodies being transferred from other Stagecoach operations in Scotland, to be joined by a dozen five-year-old L608Ds moved north from Hastings – a 600-mile journey. Other types to be allocated to Bluebird Northern in the early period of Stagecoach ownership included ECW-bodied Bristol VRTs, transferred from the group's English businesses, and new Olympians and Dennis Darts with Alexander bodies. There were also large numbers of Volvo B10Ms. The yellow Northern livery quickly gave way to Stagecoach's corporate colours. In June 1996, Bluebird Buses secured the Royal Warrant, as supplier of bus and coach services to the Royal Family at Balmoral.

In July 1991, three months after acquiring Northern, Stagecoach bought Fife, for £9.1 million, after a long

battle with Fife's management to take control of the company. The first additions to the fleet under Stagecoach were some four-year-old Renault minibuses transferred from Ribble and a trio of two-year-old Volvo Citybuses from Southdown. Like Bluebird Northern, Fife would also receive Bristol VRTs, and these were followed by large numbers of Leyland Titans transferred from Stagecoach's London companies – more than 60 by 2000. Fife had the distinction, in July 1996, of introducing the first articulated coaches to operate in Britain. These were two 18m-long Jonckheere-bodied Volvo B10Ms with 71 seats, used on the service between Anstruther and Glasgow. Low-floor buses – Dennis Dart SLFs – were introduced to Fife in 1997, and, as would happen at Bluebird Buses, these were followed by MANs.

Strathtay was sold to Yorkshire Traction in June 1991 for £1.9 million – the only SBG company to become English-owned. Its livery of orange, blue and white was retained, although the layout would be changed over time. Here too Bristol VRTs were soon in the fleet, moved north from Yorkshire Traction's English operations to replace Ailsas and older Fleetlines. Later the company would receive new Dennis Darts and Volvo Olympians. The privatised Strathtay business retrenched in the early 1990s and by 1993 had closed all three former Midland depots, at Perth, Pitlochry and Crieff. Stagecoach had won the battle of the buses in Perth.

In 2005, Strathtay became part of Stagecoach's Scottish bus interests when Stagecoach bought the Traction Group. At this time Strathtay was still operating a small number of Y-type Leopards; the last, a former Midland bus dating from 1982, survived until March 2007 – 45 years after the first Y-types entered Alexander's service. At the same time the last ex-Northern Olympians were still in use. The very last bus with an SBG association to survive with one of Alexander's successors was a 1987 Strathtay Olympian operating at Montrose depot in 2009.

The effect of all these changes, of course, was to reunite under Stagecoach ownership much of what had been the three Alexander's companies, including the entire former Fife and Northern businesses. From 2005, Stagecoach controlled operations from Elgin (and

Inverness, which prior to 1952 had briefly been part of Alexander's territory) down through Aberdeen, Dundee and Perth and into Fife. It would later take over the Rapson's business, which covered what had been Highland Omnibuses' territory to the north and west of Inverness.

The Glasgow-area operations which Midland had ceded to Kelvin in 1985 suffered badly in the early days of deregulation. Urban services, once operated by PD3s and then by Fleetlines, were being run by ex-London Routemasters. But, for all Kelvin's efforts to compete with the PTE's Strathclyde Buses business, it was struggling. It was merged with Central in 1988. There was significant retrenchment – the combined Kelvin Central fleet numbered 675, compared with 854 for the two companies just three years earlier, and would be below 500 when it was privatised in February 1991 in a management/employee buy-out. Then, in 1994, it was bought by SB Holdings, the former PTE-owned bus company which had itself been privatised in a management buy-out the previous year.

Under SB Holdings ownership the former Midland depots at Stepps and Kirkintilloch were closed, leaving only one, Cumbernauld, still in operation. FirstBus (as GRT had become in 1995 when it joined forces with Badgerline) acquired SB Holdings in June 1996, giving it control of what had been Midland's Glasgow operations along with the former Strathclyde PTE bus operations and much of what, prior to 1985, had been Central SMT's operating territory.

By 2011, First covered all of what had been Midland's territory, except for Perthshire and Oban. Former Midland depots remained in use with First at Balfron (18 buses), Bannockburn (62), Larbert (84), Linlithgow (33) and, through the First Glasgow company, Cumbernauld (75). Interestingly, both Balfron and Linlithgow, which in SBG days were running only single-deckers, now had double-deckers – Volvo Olympians at Balfron, B9TLs at Linlithgow.

Stagecoach strengthened its position in Fife when it purchased the business of Rennie's of Dunfermline – which in the late 1980s had been in competition with Fife Scottish – in 2008. Rennie's operated 50 vehicles on private-hire and contract work and remains a separate operating unit (with its own livery) within the Stagecoach group.

Stagecoach's Fife fleet in 2011 numbered 360 vehicles operating from five depots – Aberhill, Cowdenbeath, Dunfermline, Glenrothes and St Andrews, the last-named with an allocation of 30, the other four having 80-85 each. The Fife Scottish Omnibuses business – the name adopted

in 1985 still survives as the company's legal title – is part of Stagecoach East, which also controls the Strathtay Scottish operation and has a total fleet of 550 buses – the 360 in Fife plus 120 north of the Tay and 70 in Perth.

From a different perspective, when Strathtay and that part of the Bluebird Buses businesses in the former Alexander's Northern Area are taken together, Stagecoach operates 410 buses and coaches in what was once Northern territory – 120 at Strathtay and 290 at Bluebird. It still has depots in most of the towns where Alexander's had bases. So in total Stagecoach operates around 840 buses in areas which were once part of Alexander's territory, most local services being operated by low-floor buses – mainly MAN 18.220s, Dennis Darts, Alexander Dennis Enviro300s and Dennis Tridents. Older buses are Volvo Olympians, and B10Ms with Alexander PS-type bodies. Inter-urban services, which were once operated by Y-type Leopards, are covered by more than 100 Volvo B7Rs and B9Rs with Plaxton bodies fitted with wheelchair lifts. Services between Fife and Edinburgh are in part operated by the only three-axle single-deck buses in Scotland – nine 13.7m-long 56-seat Scania OmniLinks. In Perth, Stagecoach operates gold-liveried Enviro300s on one cross-city service, between Scone and Hillend, as part of a drive to attract motorists to high-quality leather-seated vehicles – a far cry from the Guy Arab IIs which

served the same route, then running between Scone and Cherrybank, 50 years ago.

Direct comparisons after 50 years are difficult. In 1961, Alexander's operated 1,937 buses and coaches. By 1985, prior to that year's reorganisation, its three successors were running 1,173. In 2011, Stagecoach and First run about 1,100 in what 50 years earlier constituted Alexander's territory.

Over that period rural services have experienced significant decline. Urban services are less comprehensive and less frequent – for example, in 1961 the most frequent Kirkcaldy town service ran every eight minutes. In 2011, the most frequent services run every 15 minutes.

On the other hand, long-distance services have grown dramatically. In 1961, Alexander's express services from Glasgow to Dundee, Aberdeen and Inverness operated only in the summer – and generally with just one journey each day in each direction, albeit with unlimited numbers of duplicates at weekends or holiday Mondays. Today Scottish Citylink, nowadays a joint venture between Stagecoach and ComfortDelGro, provides a year-round service on these and many other routes, including, for example, 16 summer weekday departures from Glasgow to Aberdeen.

Walter Alexander's name may have disappeared from Scotland's buses, but his spirit lives on.

Above **Operating on what would once have been a Northern service, a 2008 Alexander Dennis Enviro200 in the Bluebird Buses fleet leaves Inverness for Elgin in the summer of 2009. It is a 10.9m 38-seater with a Cummins ISBe engine.**
STEWART J. BROWN

Appendices

1 FLEET NUMBERING

Alexander's alphanumeric fleet–numbering system had been introduced in 1932, with single letters indicating different makes and models, and with each class being numbered from 1. Two of the original 1932 classifications survived in 1961 – P-class Tigers and R–class Leyland double–deckers. Other makes of double–decker (RO for Other) were numbered within the R series.

After World War 2 various new classes were introduced, and a two–letter system identified developments of earlier models. Thus the A series (AEC Regals) spawned AA (later AB) for 9.6–litre–engined Regal IIIs and AC for Reliances and Monocoaches.

The vehicle classifications in use in 1961 and their division between the new companies were as follows:

		FIFE	MIDLAND	NORTHERN	TOTAL
A	AEC Regal	–	15	78	93
AB	AEC Regal III 9.6–litre	–	10	–	10
AC	AEC Reliance/Monocoach	–	94	112	206
AL	Albion Valkyrie	–	–	1	1
BA	Albion Victor	5	–	–	5
C	Commer Commando	–	9	–	9
D	Daimler CVD6	–	37	4	41
E	Bristol LS6G	20	–	–	20
G	Guy Arab III	79	22	–	101
GA	Guy Arab LUF	20	–	–	20
K	Leyland Cheetah	8	3	–	11
N	Albion Nimbus	–	15	–	15
NL	Albion Aberdonian	5	1	17	23
P	Leyland Tiger TS series	40	82	49	171
PA	Leyland Tiger PS1	45	94	60	199
PB	Leyland Tiger OPS2	10	6	4	20
PC	Leyland Royal Tiger	11	57	16	84
PD	Leyland Tiger Cub	57	137	10	204
R*	Leyland Titan TD series	12	65	16	93
RA*	Leyland Titan PD1	–	48	26	74
RB*	Leyland Titan PD2/PD3	26	115	42	183
RC	AEC Regent III	–	20	2	22
RD	Bristol Lodekka	80	72	–	152
RO*	Guy Arab/Daimler CWA6	98	40	10	148
W	Bedford	–	25	7	32
		516	**967**	**454**	**1,937**

*The R and RO classes were numbered in a common series, as were the RA and RB classes.

The simple approach to renumbering adopted by the three new companies – adding an appropriate F, M or N prefix to the existing numbers – meant that at each company within any particular series there were many gaps, except where an entire class passed to one of the new companies. Five classes passed intact to one or other of the new companies. These were the 10 AB-class Regals and 15 N-class Albion Nimbuses, which went to Midland, and the five BA–class Albion Victors, 20 E-class Bristols and 20 GA-class Guys, which went to Fife. It was also possible to find what had been consecutively numbered vehicles in the original Alexander's fleet now under different ownership – for example, three Tiger PS1s which had been Alexander's PA7–9 became FPA7, MPA8 and NPA9 in the Fife, Midland and Northern fleets respectively.

From 1962 onwards, when new buses of existing types were delivered they were numbered after the highest example in each fleet. Thus in 1962 new Lodekkas for Fife were numbered from FRD153, while those for Midland took numbers from MRD161. These followed on from the former Fife Area's RD152 and the former Southern Area's RD160.

Where new types were introduced, all three companies would until the 1980s use the same vehicle type code – eg RE for Albion Lowlanders, NV for Albion Vikings – but each with their own series of numbers. Thus there were buses numbered FRE1, MRE1 and NRE1.

Left **Towards the ends of their lives Y-type coaches were downgraded to bus work and were repainted in bus livery by all three Alexander's companies. This is a 1969 Albion Viking – the last to be delivered to Midland – in Springburn in 1981. The operation of Vikings by Midland ended in 1982. All three Alexander's companies used the classification NV for Albion Vikings.** STEWART J. BROWN

New type classifications introduced after the creation of the three new companies were:

FIFE

FAC	AEC Reliance	1962
FLT	Leyland Tiger/Royal Tiger Doyen	1983
FM	Minibus (Renault S56)	1987
FNV	Albion Viking	1965
FPE	Leyland Leopard	1970
FPN	Leyland National	1978
FRA	Ailsa/Volvo Citybus	1975
FRE	Albion Lowlander	1963
FRF	Daimler Fleetline	1968
FRN	Leyland Atlantean (ex-Grampian)	1984
FRO	Leyland Olympian	1983
FT	Ford	1974
FV	Volvo B10M (ex-Western)	1987
FW	Bedford	1962

MIDLAND

MLH	Bristol LH	1970
MMB*	Minibus (Mercedes-Benz L608D, ex-Kelvin)	1987
MMM*	Minibus (MCW Metrorider)	1987
MMS*	Minibus (Freight Rover Sherpa)	1986
MNA	Albion (various models, ex-Carmichael)	1966
MNV	Albion Viking	1965
MPE	Leyland Leopard	1965
MPF	Leyland Worldmaster (ex-Carmichael)	1966
MPN	Leyland National	1978
MPT	Leyland Tiger	1983
MRA	Ailsa	1977
MRE	Albion Lowlander	1963
MRF	Daimler Fleetline	1967
MRM	MCW Metrobus	1979
MRO	Leyland Olympian (demonstrator)	1980
MRT	Bristol VRT	1970
MSE	Seddon Pennine	1985
MT	Ford	1974

* All three minibus types numbered in a common series

NORTHERN

NA	Volvo B57	1983
NAB	AEC Regal IV	1965
NBT†	Leyland Tiger bus	1983
NCT†	Leyland Tiger coach	1983
NLT†	Leyland Tiger London coach	1982
NRT†	Leyland Royal Tiger Doyen	1984
NCM*	MCW Metroliner (single-deck)	1984
NDM*	MCW Metroliner (double-deck)	1982
ND	Dennis Lancet	1982
NE	Bristol LWL (ex-Mitchell)	1967
NF	Foden (ex-Strachan's)	1965
NGA	Guy Arab LUF (ex-Mitchell)	1967
NLO	Leyland Olympian	1981
NM	Minibus (various models)	1989
NNV	Albion Viking	1965
NPE	Leyland Leopard	1965
NPN	Leyland National	1980
NRD	Bristol Lodekka (ex-Midland)	1979
NRE	Albion Lowlander	1963
NRF	Daimler Fleetline	1976
NT	Ford	1966
NX	Limousines	1967

† All four Tiger types numbered in a common series

* Metroliner types numbered in a common series

Prior to 1961, fleet numbers were generally displayed on cast metal plates on the front (and on the bonnet side of half-cab vehicles). On the rear there would be either a cast plate or a transfer. Fife used hand-painted rather than cast plates until 1978, when it started using transfers. Midland and Northern continued using cast metal plates until switching to transfers from 1970 and 1976 respectively.

Left **Each spring Alexander's hosted a one-day coach show in Dundas Street bus station to create interest among potential holiday-tour customers, and this practice was continued by Midland for a few years. This is the 1964 event. Nearest the camera are two Bedford VASs, alongside two Tiger Cubs, a 1963 Y-type and a 1961 38-seat touring coach. The last two vehicles are from the Scottish Omnibuses and Western SMT fleets. The photograph was taken from the upper deck of a bus halted by the bus station entrance.** STEWART J. BROWN

2 DEPOT CODES

Depot		Allocation, January 1966	Notes
FIFE			
A	Anstruther	26	closed 1981
AL	Aberhill	71	still in use with Stagecoach
C	Cowdenbeath	47	still in use with Stagecoach
CR	Cupar	30	closed 1981
D	Dunfermline	125	still in use with Stagecoach
D2	Dunfermline Market Street	–	closed 1961
G	Glenrothes (opened 1985)	–	still in use with Stagecoach
K	Kirkcaldy	124	non–operational from 2004
KY	Kelty	43	closed 1979
LY	Lochgelly	30	closed 1982
N	Newburgh	13	closed by Stagecoach 1991
STA	St Andrews	12	still in use with Stagecoach
	TOTAL	**521**	
MIDLAND			
A	Alloa	60	closed by GRT, 1991
B	Balfron	28	still in use with First
BN	Bannockburn	57	still in use with First
C	Crieff	27	to Strathtay, closed 1991
CD	Cumbernauld	–	still in use with First
CL	Callander	–	outstation of Stirling from 1965
G	Grangemouth	91	closed 1988
K	Kilsyth	61	to Kelvin, closed 1988
KH	Kirkintilloch	87	to Kelvin, closed 1995
L	Larbert	119	still in use with First
LW	Linlithgow (from 1985)	–	still in use with First
M	Milngavie	120	to Kelvin, closed 1987
ON	Oban	16	to Oban & District, relocated
P	Perth	81	to Strathtay, closed 1993
PY	Pitlochry	11	to Strathtay, closed 1993
S	Stirling	84	closed 1983
SS	Stepps	117	to Kelvin, closed 1995
	TOTAL	**959**	

Depot		Allocation, January 1966	Notes
NORTHERN			
A	Aberdeen	119	relocated by Stagecoach
AH	Arbroath	20	to Strathtay, still in use
B	Buckie	10	closed
BL	Blairgowrie	17	to Strathtay, still in use
C	City service, Aberdeen (from 1983)	–	
D	Dundee	65	to Strathtay, relocated 2008
E	Elgin	55	still in use with Stagecoach
F	Fyvie	6	outstation of Aberdeen, 1975
F	Fraserburgh (from 1975)	–	still in use with Stagecoach
FR	Forfar	21	to Strathtay, still in use
H	Huntly	6	outstation of Elgin, 1980
M	Montrose	21	to Strathtay, still in use
MF	Macduff	22	still in use with Stagecoach
P	Peterhead	26	relocated by Stagecoach
R	Rosehearty	16	closed 1975
S	Stonehaven	26	relocated by Stagecoach
	TOTAL	**430**	

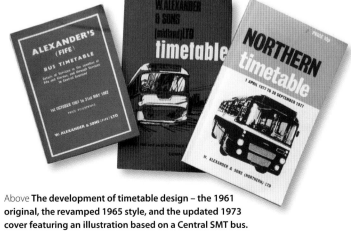

Above **The development of timetable design – the 1961 original, the revamped 1965 style, and the updated 1973 cover featuring an illustration based on a Central SMT bus.**

STEWART J. BROWN